T0245793

A HIKER'S GUIDE TO THE

BARTRAM NATIONAL
RECREATION TRAIL

IN GEORGIA AND *NORTH CAROLINA*

A HIKER'S GUIDE TO THE

Bartram National Recreation Trail

IN *GEORGIA* AND *NORTH CAROLINA*

Brent Martin

MILESTONE PRESS
AN IMPRINT OF
THE UNIVERSITY OF GEORGIA PRESS
ATHENS

© 2024 by the University of Georgia Press
Athens, Georgia 30602
www.ugapress.org
All rights reserved
Designed by Kaelin Chappell Broaddus
Set in 10.5/13.5 Bodoni Egyptian Pro
by Kaelin Chappell Broaddus
Printed and bound by Sheridan Books, Inc.
The paper in this book meets the guidelines for permanence and
durability of the Committee on Production Guidelines for
Book Longevity of the Council on Library Resources.

Most University of Georgia Press titles are
available from popular e-book vendors.

Printed in the United States of America
28 27 26 25 24 P 5 4 3 2 1

Library of Congress Cataloging-in-Publication Data

Names: Martin, Brent, author.
Title: A hiker's guide to the Bartram National Recreation Trail in
        Georgia and North Carolina / Brent Martin.
Description: Athens : Milestone Press, an imprint of the University of
        Georgia Press, [2024] | Includes bibliographical references.
Identifiers: LCCN 2023040789 | ISBN 9781889596426 (paperback : alk. paper)
Subjects: LCSH: Hiking—Bartram Trail (Ga. and N.C.)—Guidebooks. |
        Walking—Bartram Trail (Ga. and N.C.)—Guidebooks. | Natural
        history—Southern States. | Georgia—Description and travel. |
        North Carolina—Description and travel. | Bartram, William, 1739–1823
        —Travel—Southern States.
Classification: LCC GV199.42.G46 M37 2024 | DDC 796.5109756/9—dc23/eng/20231024
LC record available at https://lccn.loc.gov/2023040789

CONTENTS

ACKNOWLEDGMENTS

There would be no Bartram Trail without the visionary found-
ers of the Georgia and North Carolina Bartram Trail Societies,
which merged in 2021 to form the Blue Ridge Bartram Trail Conservancy. These early volunteers began the hard work of planning, mapping, building, and maintaining this trail almost 50
years ago. Grady Bell and Walter McKelvey first envisioned a
Georgia/North Carolina Bartram Trail in the early 1970s. They
were joined in their efforts by the extraordinary botanist Dr. Dan
Pittillo, a professor emeritus of Western Carolina University. We
owe a debt of gratitude to the many volunteers who offer their
time maintaining the trail, but over the years several individuals have provided leadership in this effort, including Jim Chance,
Tim Warren, and John Ray. John Ray and Malcolm Skove were
the first to map the trail and create the spiral-bound guidebooks
that have been an invaluable resource for Bartram Trail hikers
since their first printing in 2001. Ray and Skove used a distance
measuring wheel, as well as a handheld GPS unit, refining the
distances and maps over the years with each new printing.

Ancient trails expert Lamar Marshall created the maps for
this book and added rich cultural context and insights. His un-
paralleled understanding of how humans traveled across this
landscape for centuries is an invaluable resource, as well as an
example for those wanting to have a deep connection to place. I
extend my deepest gratitude to the North Carolina Arts Council
for providing funding for this mapping effort, and to my friends
who helped in some direct way along this trail guide journey:
Craig Burkhalter, John Lane, Helen Meadors, Kristian Under-
wood, Melanie and Keith Vickers, the Blue Ridge Bartram Trail

Conservancy, Outdoor 76—and my stalwart comrade in all things wild for thirty years, Angela Faye Martin. I would also like to thank the many dedicated Bartramites who section hiked the trail with me each month during the pandemic years of 2020 and 2021, listening to me ramble on about Bartram and the many interesting features of, as Bartram described it, this "magnificent landscape, infinitely varied, and without bound."

A HIKER'S GUIDE TO THE
BARTRAM NATIONAL RECREATION TRAIL
IN *GEORGIA* AND *NORTH CAROLINA*

INTRODUCTION

I first encountered the name of William Bartram some years ago while living and working in the northwest Georgia mountains. I was attempting a dissertation on land use patterns in the area, studying maps and journals of the Georgia Surveyor General's Office that had resulted from preparations in the 1830s for the brutal removal of the Cherokee people and the subsequent carving up and doling out of their historic homeland to settlers. Bartram did not travel into the northwest Georgia mountains, but I read portions of his journals out of curiosity and to familiarize myself with his impressions of the mountains that lie farther to the east. I was also working for a conservation organization at the time, and Bartram's name was being bantered about during the creation of a new forest management plan for the Chattahoochee National Forest, a plan that took almost a decade to complete. Some of the other people at the planning table had used his landscape descriptions to argue for more intensive management of our forests. Their argument was based on his observations of open and grassy forests, vast upland and lowland meadows, and open fields of strawberries. Bartram was describing a Cherokee landscape that was managed by humans through fire and clearing, as well by thousands of beavers, elk, bison, and passenger pigeons—species that would be eradicated from the landscape in the years to come, in some cases permanently. Though it seemed to be an argument for managing backward in time, it was nonetheless interesting, and when I moved to Cowee Valley near Franklin, North Carolina, in 2003, these landscape descriptions provided a much deeper connection to place for me, as did the fact that there was a Bartram Trail here and an organization that worked to maintain it and promote Bartram's importance in American history.

Though Bartram was a significant information source for my interest in the cultural and natural history of the Chattooga and Little Tennessee watersheds, he also became a significant inspirational source. Here was someone who, in stark contrast to the colonial settlers of his day, valued humility before all of creation as an essential trait and regarded the American landscape for its beauty and magnificence over its utility and capacity for extraction and conquest. He was a rare individual who rejected the norms of his day and chose instead to devote his life to the study of nature, and who lived somewhat as an outsider following the years of his travels, avoiding recognition and fame. Remarkably, over 200 years later, we still remember him for this.

Why a Bartram National Recreation Trail?

The 112-mile-long Bartram National Recreation Trail loosely follows the route that the 18th-century naturalist and artist William Bartram (1739-1823) traveled in the spring of 1775. Bartram had journeyed through parts of the Southeast in the 1760s with his botanist father, John, who was on a royal mission for King George III to assess and describe lands acquired by England following the French and Indian War. The Bartrams were Philadelphia Quakers and at the time had one of the most significant plant businesses in colonial America. John was renowned in England for his plant knowledge and collection, and William was equally talented and determined to continue in his father's line of work. William was a bit of a dreamer, with an artist's soul and a scientific mind. His 1791 account of his journeys through the wilds of the Southeast, *Travels through North and South Carolina, Georgia, East and West Florida, the Cherokee Country, the Extensive Territories of the Muscogulges or Creek Confederacy, and the Country of the Chactaws*, is an amalgamation of the scientific thinking and language of his day and the effusive and rhapsodic language of the emerging Romantic era in literature. The English poets William Wordsworth and Samuel Taylor Coleridge were influenced by Bartram's imagery and thinking, and *Travels* became highly popular in Europe during the first decade of the 19th century.

William Bartram could be considered one of America's first creative nonfiction nature writers—as well as America's first hippie. He was the first colonial American to romanticize the American landscape, and the historian Roderick Nash credits Bartram as the first to describe it with the term *sublime*. This romanticization could also be considered a foundation of the conservation ethic in America, Bartram being followed by Henry David Thoreau and Ralph Waldo Emerson in the mid-19th century, the Hudson River School of landscape painting, and later John Muir and John Burroughs. Let us also remember that the American landscape had been settled and appreciated for thousands of years by native peoples with their own ethics and languages, and that Bartram was influenced by these ethics and articulated them in his writings.

William fell in love with Florida's St. Johns River valley while exploring with his father, and though reluctant to do so, John Bartram set his son up as a rice planter there, an endeavor at which William failed miserably. Following this failure, William returned to Philadelphia, where he attempted various business endeavors at his father's behest, all the while wanting to pursue botany and art. One of the Bartram family's most significant patrons was the British textile merchant Peter Collinson. Collinson had shown William's artwork to various plant collectors in England, and one of them, the British doctor John Fothergill, offered William the financing to explore the Southeast more extensively than he and his father had in the mid-1760s.

Under Fothergill's patronage, Bartram explored the southeastern colonies of British North America from 1773 to 1777. His task was to describe and collect species yet unknown to science, as well as to illustrate these findings. He was a talented observer and communicator, and though funded primarily for his plant collections, he also provided a detailed and sympathetic account of Native American customs and villages and the traits of individuals he encountered.

The Bartrams had not ventured into Appalachia during their earlier explorations. William's journey into the mountains was the first of its kind, as it was a mission born not of a desire to trade, convert, or exploit but of curiosity and wonder. His route began in Charleston, South Carolina, on the Charles Town trade path, which traveled through the then-destroyed Lower Town Cherokee villages in South Carolina and into the mountains near the Cherokee village of Stekoe. From there he traveled across the Eastern Continental Divide into the Little Tennessee River Valley, home of the Middle Town Cherokees.

Previous ventures into the southern mountains had been military or economic in nature, with two campaigns of the French and Indian War having been fought in 1760 and 1761 in the Little Tennessee River Valley. In Bartram's recounting of his entry into the mountains, he describes some of the Cherokee villages that never recovered from these two campaigns. His destination was Cowee, the diplomatic and commercial center of the Middle Town Cherokees, and his are the only detailed descriptions of the village before it was destroyed beyond recovery in one of the early campaigns of the American Revolution in the summer of 1776.

Throughout his explorations, Bartram documented the local flora and fauna, along with the landscape, and he wrote notable historical accounts and descriptions of the villages and customs of the Middle Town Cherokees. His *Travels* was published in 1791 and was eventually translated into multiple languages, and its significance remains profound. Bartram was the first American to provide such rhapsodic and historical accounts of the landscape, and he was the first contributor to a postrevolutionary American natural and environmental history. Two hundred years later, a consortium of states convened to commemorate the bicentennial of his travels, resulting in a network of historical markers, interpretive walks, and trails, as well as a commitment to keeping William Bartram alive in the public consciousness.

The north Georgia / North Carolina Bartram Trail was one result of this consortium, and since that time the trail's popularity and use have grown, the result being that Bartram's legacy has remained vibrant and relevant in the areas he traveled. The trail begins in Georgia along the Chattooga River (federally designated a wild and scenic river in 1974), whence it meanders

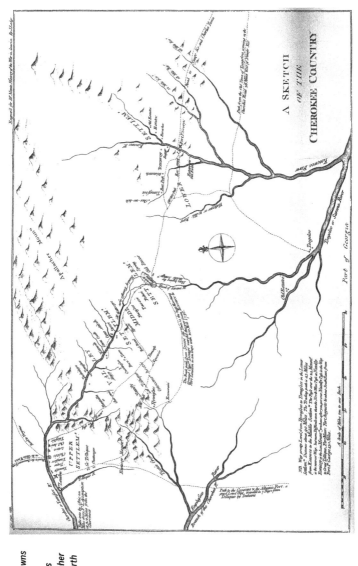

Trade paths and Cherokee towns during the 1760–1761 French and Indian War campaigns as mapped by British cartographer Thomas Mante. Courtesy North Carolina State Archives.

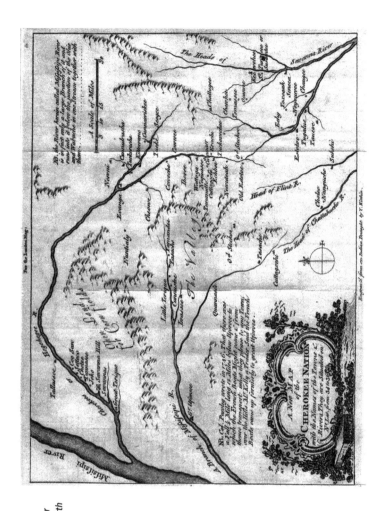

1760 map of the Cherokee Nation by British cartographer Thomas Kitchin. Courtesy North Carolina State Archives.

through the Chattahoochee National Forest, crossing the North Carolina state line into the Nantahala National Forest. Once into the Nantahala, the trail traverses the Fishhawk Mountains, descends into the Little Tennessee River Valley, and then climbs from the town of Franklin, North Carolina, up and over the Nantahala Mountains, where it merges with the Appalachian Trail for over a mile before descending into the Nantahala Gorge. Once into the gorge, it makes a steep ascent of Cheoah Bald, where it rejoins the Appalachian Trail near its terminus at the summit.

What to Expect on the Trail

The Bartram Trail varies greatly in topography and elevation. Depending on the section they're embarking on, hikers must prepare for stream crossings, steep elevation gains and losses, uneven and rocky terrain, lack of water, rapidly changing weather conditions, or all of the above. Temperatures are cooler at the higher elevations, and summer rains can leave a hiker chilled to the point of hypothermia if caught unprepared. Winter can include crisp, bright, warm days followed by subfreezing temperatures, snow, and/or ice. The Bartram Trail passes through a high rainfall area, with over 100 inches of rain in a year not uncommon. The trail also increases in difficulty as it enters North Carolina and heads into higher elevations and more rugged terrain.

From the trail's beginning along the Chattooga River at 1,600 feet, there is little elevation gain until the trail's westward departure toward Warwoman Creek and Earls Ford. At Earls Ford the trail climbs and proceeds onto Sandy Ford. At Sandy Ford the trail leaves the river corridor and contours around several peaks (such as Rainy Mountain), climbing and descending, with the ultimate elevation gain in Georgia at Rabun Bald (4,695 feet), where the trail descends and heads to the North Carolina state line. The Georgia sections are lower in elevation than the North Carolina sections and in general are less difficult. Longer hikes are therefore possible, and there is also more access to water. As the trail leaves Georgia, traveling through the headwaters of Overflow Creek and the Overflow Wilderness Study Area, it climbs the spine of the Fishhawk mountain range to Scaly Mountain—a rocky bald with one of the best views along the Bartram Trail—and then follows the ridgeline down for almost 14 miles to Hickory Knoll Road.

From the Hickory Knoll Road parking area to the Macon County Fairgrounds, the trail is a 7-mile road walk without sidewalks. The setting is pastoral and pleasant enough but is nonetheless busy for a rural area, and utmost caution should be used while walking the often narrow shoulders. After reaching the fairgrounds, the trail enters the parking area, where a kiosk is located at the trail's crossing of Cartoogechaye Creek. From there, hikers follow the beautiful Cartoogechaye Creek and Little Tennessee River for an easy and pleasant 4 miles through the Macon County Recreation Park and along the Little Tennessee River Greenway; this new section of trail eliminates the crossing of US 441 and US 64. Upon reaching the greenway's Big Bear Shelter, the trail leaves the greenway and proceeds west on Main Street, passing the historic Nikwasi Mound and traveling through downtown Franklin. The trail then continues on Old Murphy Road to Pressley Road and the Wallace Branch trailhead.

Hikers might also consider canoeing or kayaking from Hickory Knoll Road to Tassee Shelter on the greenway near downtown Franklin. This 7-mile river section begins at the public put-in on Riverside Drive, a mile from the Hickory Knoll trailhead, and is a fairly gentle paddle, with no difficult water to navigate. The Blue Ridge Bartram Trail Conservancy annually clears this section of blowdowns, but be forewarned that there could be portages and low water to navigate during dry spells. See the Additional Resources section at the end of this guide for further information.

The 11-mile hike from Wallace Branch to Wayah Bald is the most difficult hike on the Bartram Trail, regardless of the direction you are traveling. South to north, the trail ascends Trimont Ridge and then crosses a series of small peaks before the long 5-mile climb up to the summit of Wayah Bald (5,342 ft), the highest point on the Bartram Trail. The trail then joins the Appalachian Trail before descending, steeply at times, to Lake Nantahala, where a short road walk takes hikers to the next trailhead at the old Phillips 66 gas station. The next 15 miles of trail are not difficult, passing the Nantahala Dam and following a rural gravel road to Appletree Campground. From Appletree, the trail parallels the Nantahala River before leaving the river and traveling along a relatively moderate and contoured grade through the mountains, and then descending for over a mile on a Duke Energy access road to Beechertown. From Beechertown, the trail follows US 19N for a mile before beginning the 5.5-mile ascent (with an approximate 3,000 feet of elevation gain) to Cheoah Bald, the second-highest point on the trail at 5,062 feet. At the trail's northern terminus, hikers have the option of returning to the Beechertown trailhead, hiking another 5 miles north on the Appalachian Trail to Stecoah Gap, or hiking 8 miles on the Appalachian Trail to Nantahala Outdoor Center.

Whether planning a day hike on the Bartram Trail or an extended backpacking trip, consider your abilities for elevation gain and the associated distances, as these are two major factors in enjoying your hike. Many of the Bartram sections are also easier to travel north to south, as there is a general loss of elevation as one proceeds south, particularly in Georgia. Regardless, if you are not an experienced hiker, start with hikes under five miles, and check the Blue Ridge Bartram Trail Conservancy website at www.blueridgebartram.org for information on trail conditions.

Less experienced hikers might also benefit from hiking more popular sections, where access is easier, and where they might feel more comfortable knowing that there are other hikers close by to answer questions about logistics, trail conditions, and so on. Most of the major access points for the trail in North Carolina have informational kiosks, and the planning and construction of kiosks for the Georgia sections is underway.

Basic Safety Precautions

Regardless of your hike location on the Bartram Trail, certain safety precautions should always be taken. The Bartram Trail is marked with rectangular yellow blazes, with double blazes indicating a potentially confusing turn or an intersection with another trail. Pay attention to the blazes and you'll be fine. Blue blazes represent side trails. Know where you're going! Many hikers now depend on trail apps for their journeys, but apps are not always reliable, nor are batteries. Paper maps with contour lines and local features do not need batteries, nor do they produce questionable locations or results. Maps are also more visually interesting and create a stronger sense of confidence on the trail. Always let someone know your location and hike details, particularly if you are hiking alone. This goes for groups as well, regardless of their size. When hiking with larger groups it is also important to assign a sweep—someone who will bring up the rear of the group and who can ensure that everyone is accounted for and moving forward.

Southern Appalachian weather can change dramatically, and one should always prepare for whatever extremes might emerge. Even on summer days when the forecast is warm and there is only the slightest chance of rain, a rain jacket, a change of socks, and an extra layer are important accessories. Winter hikes are trickier, and it is always a good idea to layer clothing, prepare for the forecast, and expect it to be worse than predicted. Ask yourself if you have what you might need to survive a night on the trail should an emergency arise. Always bring a map, a good first-aid kit, fire starter, a flashlight, and a little extra food for any hike that is expected to take you a full day to complete.

Although the likelihood of encountering a bear is low, such occurrences are on the increase in areas popular with campers, where food is often left out or left behind in campfire rings or around campsites. The Bartram Trail has no designated campsites, and all the camping is dispersed. Practice Leave No Trace (www.lnt.org) when you camp to ensure that other campers using your site are at less risk. Bear spray can also provide some security in the rare event of a dangerous bear-human encounter. If overnighting, always hang food a good distance from your tent, and utilize bear canisters to keep your food and beverages safe and to control odor. The websites for the North Carolina national forests (www.fs.usda.gov/nfsnc) and Georgia's Chattahoochee-Oconee National Forest (www.fs.usda.gov/conf) list bear advisories, and you can also find excellent backcountry bear information at www.bearsmart.com; be sure to consult these resources and plan accordingly.

Purify your drinking water. You might be looking at what appears to be a pure mountain stream, but the microscopic parasite Giardia could be present. Giardia is transferred to water through the fecal matter of wild animals and can cause serious gastrointestinal problems. Much of the Giardia present in mountain streams originates from wild hogs—an increasing problem on the Bartram Trail, particularly within the Appletree section. Simple purification through a variety of modern backcountry options such as UV treatment, water filter straws, and iodine tablets works fine, or you can always resort to the old-fashioned method of boiling water at a full boil for two minutes.

Be aware that you could be hiking during hunting season. The timing of hunting seasons depends on the game animal and the state, but in general hunting seasons begin in early autumn and extend through February. There is also a spring season for turkey hunting. If you wear bright colors or an orange cap to ensure that hunters can see you, you'll be fine. Most hunters avoid trails, knowing that hikers can disrupt hunting, but you can never be too safe. Check the state game regulations online if you're especially concerned.

There are multiple bridges out on the Bartram Trail in Georgia. Streams are easily forded in mild weather, and none of the crossings are difficult to wade. Heavy rains can swell streams quickly, however, and caution should be used at some of the larger streams, such as Dicks Creek. These bridges are scheduled to be replaced and upgraded by the Forest Service in 2024.

Accessing the trail via Forest Service roads can also be a problem, particularly in winter; many roads close in December and do not reopen until mid-March. Check the Forest Service websites for road closures, or call the district ranger office for the most up-to-date information.

Bartram artwork from the John Fothergill collection,
Natural History Museum, London

Bartram artwork from the John Fothergill collection,
Natural History Museum, London

PART I

Georgia

Highway 28 to Sandy Ford Road

(9.5 MILES)

Crossed a delightful river, the main branch of Tugilo, when I began to ascend again, first over swelling turfy ridges, varied with groves of stately forest trees, then ascending again more steep, grassy hill sides, rested on the top of mount Magnolia, which appeared to me to be the highest ridge of the Cherokee mountains, which separates the waters of Savanna river from those of the Tanase or great main branch of the Cherokee river.

Cultural and Natural History

Bartram entered the northeast Georgia mountains in May 1775 via the old Charles Town trade path, a route that had been used by colonial traders and military campaigns for almost 100 years and by Native Americans before that. Bartram had departed Charles Town (Charleston) for Cherokee country on April 22, 1775, arriving at Oconee Mountain near modern-day Oconee State Park around May 19 and then crossing the Chattooga River soon after at Earls Ford. From there he followed Warwoman Creek toward modern-day Clayton and what was then the abandoned Cherokee village of Stekoe. He described Martin Creek Falls and crossed the Blue Ridge Divide at Courthouse Gap, recording his observations of species new to 18th-century botany, such as Fraser magnolia. This is the standard interpretation of his route, but cartographer and ancient trails expert Lamar

Marshall has recently presented a more likely route, based on a much deeper analysis of Bartram's descriptions of the landscape in his *Travels* and of the ancient pathways that traversed the landscape. According to Marshall, Bartram left the Charles Town trade path near the abandoned Cherokee town of Oconee in the Blue Ridge foothills and followed what was known as the Station Road to Chattooga Old Town.

The Station Road was an old Cherokee trail that connected Chattooga Old Town to Oconee Town. This route has Bartram crossing the Chattooga closer to where the Bartram Trail actually begins today at Russell Bridge. From there he would have followed the Cherokee trail along what is now Highway 28 up to what may have been Satulah Mountain. Marshall's analysis is hard to dispute. Bartram describes crossing "Falling Creek" twice, which has always stumped historians but which would make sense if he traveled up to the Highlands Plateau and descended the established trade path down to the Chattooga. Bartram states that after he crossed the "main branch of Tugilo," he began to ascend "steep, grassy hill sides" until he reached what he describes as the "highest ridge of the Cherokee mountains." Descending the other side, he saw before him "a level plain supporting a grand high forest and groves." This does not fit the description of what would be seen from Pinnacle Knob, on which Bartram is historically believed to have been at the time.

Bartram named the peak "mount Magnolia," after the trees that flourished all around him. He had first encountered Fraser magnolias earlier while traveling into the mountains, and this new species of magnolia he named *Magnolia auriculata*. The absence of the species on Pinnacle Knob is another consideration in favor of Marshall's analysis. Marshall also makes the point that as Bartram crossed the Chattooga, he described the abandoned Cherokee village known now as Chattooga Old Town. There was no such village at Earls Ford, giving further credence to the route proposed by Marshall. However, regardless of the route Bartram actually took, the Bartram Trail today in Georgia follows ancient travel routes that he may well have used.

Another interesting dimension to this area's history is the river itself. The Chattooga was made famous by James Dickey's classic novel *Deliverance* (1970) and the subsequent film adaptation released in 1972. The movie's critical acclaim and commercial success led to the Chattooga becoming a highly popular destination, attracting inexperienced boaters who descended the dangerous river with little skill or experience, with many trips ending in death. Its federal designation as a wild and scenic river in 1974 ensured protection of its natural condition, and as you walk the Bartram from its beginning, you will see no development along the river's shores, which is uncommon among most Appalachian streams of this size today. It is truly a wild river, and despite the microplastics, the alterations from logging over the last century, and the roads lacing through the landscape, the Chattooga is still as rugged and awe inspiring as when Bartram encountered it in 1775 and when Dickey first encountered it in the early 1970s.

Dickey was an admirer of Bartram and contributed the introduction to a 1988 Penguin edition of Bartram's *Travels*. Dickey wrote that "few writers can give us, as Bartram does, the sense of this continually emerging wholeness, of the essential unity of nature—broken only where we break it—in all its multifarious magnitude, its swarming, direct and mysterious promise, and we may still, anytime we wish, open our eyes to it with Bartram, where at dawn over Georgia and Florida the sun is new every day, and light falls with the sure and daring creativity of God's imagination, full on the 'wondrous machine.'" These are great thoughts to carry with you as you begin your journey on the Bartram Trail.

Section Overview

Access: The Bartram Trail begins on the Georgia/South Carolina state line where the Chattooga River runs under GA 28 and Russell Bridge. To access the trailhead from Clayton, travel east on Warwoman Road from US 441 for 14.0 miles to its terminus at 28 and turn right. Travel south for 2.0 miles on 28, and the parking area will be on your left, just before the highway crosses the bridge. Near the information kiosk, you'll see a large granite boulder that is engraved *Bartram Trail, Warwoman Dell, 19*.

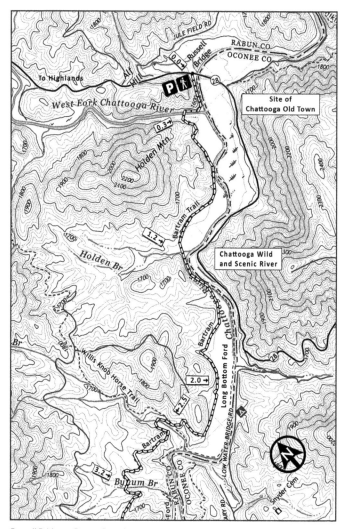

Russell Bridge to Bynum Branch

The trail begins across the road and parallels the Chattooga until it turns toward the Chattooga's West Fork and a bridge crossing, with great views of the confluence downstream.

0.0 (elevation 1,580 ft). From Russell Bridge on the South Carolina state line, the trail follows the West Fork of the Chattooga on an old roadbed for 0.3 mile before crossing the West Fork on a suspension bridge. The confluence of the West Fork and the

North Fork of the Chattooga can be seen 100 yards downstream, forming the main stem of the Chattooga River.

0.3 Cross the West Fork of the Chattooga River via the suspension bridge and turn left toward the main stem of the Chattooga. Where the trail turns left, a side trail to the right leads to decent campsites. The trail roughly parallels the river downstream for the next 0.9 mile, past the site of the ancient Cherokee village named Chattooga Old Town on the opposite side of the river. This was also the site of the historic Russell Farm, where lodgers from warmer regions stayed in the late 19th and early 20th centuries on their way to the cooler environment of Highlands, NC. The forest is recovering cutover farmland dominated by white pines and mountain laurel and increasingly choked with invasive species such as privet and multiflora rose.

1.2 Cross Holden Branch on a wooden footbridge and climb up to an old roadbed, once again paralleling the river, though the river is not visible due to dense pine forest. After 0.2 mile, the boat launch that marks the beginning of Section II for paddlers is visible across the river.

2.0 The remains of an old hay baler will appear on your left. This is the site of the old Holden farm; what is left of the farmhouse chimney is off the trail to the right. Dense privet and multiflora rose are choking native habitat and species along this section, so expect dense growth. Though the Bartram Trail Conservancy brush-cuts this section as often as possible, it can be a dense tangle to walk through during the wet summer months. A large mulberry tree and numerous black walnut trees are mixed in with white pines, signs of the clearing that once existed here. Daffodils can be seen blooming here in the early spring. For more adventurous hikers, the Holden Cemetery, dating to 1850, is off-trail some 100 yards uphill from the chimney and is well worth the visit.

2.5 The Bartram joins a horse trail that begins on Willis Knob Road and then soon crosses Adline Branch on a footbridge. During high water the Chattooga can back up Adline Branch and flood the bridge, but bushwhacking upstream a short distance provides opportunities to cross the branch and bushwhack back to the trail. You will pass a good campsite to the left after cross-

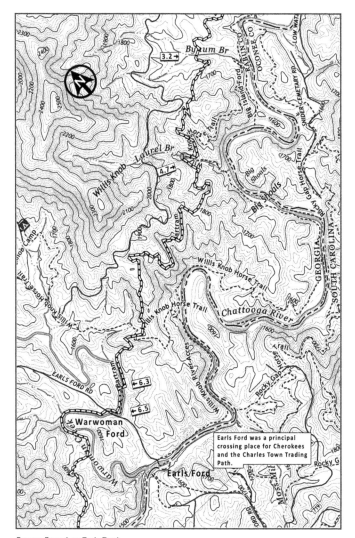

Bynum Branch to Earls Ford

ing the bridge. Horse trails coming off Willis Knob Road in this area are marked with green diamond blazes. Pay attention to blazes as you hike to Sandy Ford and make sure you are on the Bartram with its rectangular yellow blazes.

3.2 Cross Bynum Branch on the footbridge. A good campsite appears shortly on the left.

4.7 Bear left, as another horse trail continues straight.

6.3 Cross Warwoman Creek on a 66-foot metal footbridge. Turn left after crossing. Multiple campsites are ahead along Warwoman Creek.

6.5 Reach Earls Ford Road, which is gravel and deeply incised. The ancient ford across Warwoman Creek where Bartram is believed to have crossed is just to your left. Although the ford features campsites, one must be prepared for weekend revelry and a host of people who enjoy crossing the stream with ATVs and large jeeps and trucks. It's best to move on, particularly on a weekend, to nearby campsites away from the road. Walk 30 feet north and to your right up Earls Ford Road, then turn left at the large, engraved Bartram Trail stone. Earls Ford Road continues for 3.1 miles to Warwoman Road. To access this area by vehicle, travel east on Warwoman Road from US 441 in Clayton for 8.1 miles and turn right onto Earls Ford Road.

6.5 Meander for 0.6 mile along Warwoman Creek before merging onto an old road above it and departing the creek, traveling through a young hardwood forest until reaching the Chattooga River at 7.8 miles.

7.8 For the next half-mile, the trail parallels the Chattooga, arguably the most spectacular stretch of Georgia's section of the Bartram Trail, with several good campsites. You are now on Section III of the Chattooga Wild and Scenic River.

8.3 An old road leads down to a campsite along the river, after which the trail bears right and uphill, leaving the Chattooga. It is somewhat easy to miss this turn, so if you find yourself down by the river with no yellow blazes in sight, turn around and head back up, away from the river. Travel now through storm-damaged hardwood forest on the uphill side. For the next 0.8 mile there are a few decent campsites.

9.1 Reach the side trail to Dicks Creek Falls and the Chattooga River. There is a short bridge visible to the left where the trail leaves the Bartram. It is well worth the additional half-mile round trip walk to see this beautiful 60-foot waterfall as it drops and cascades into an equally beautiful section of the Chattooga.

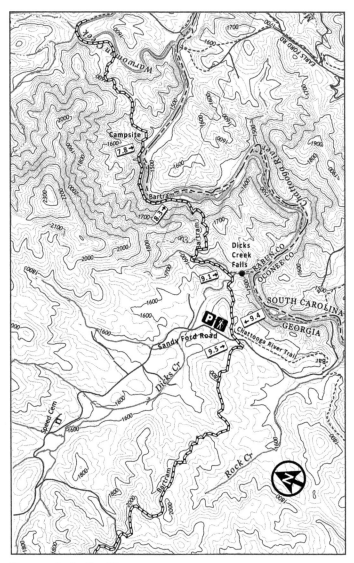

Warwoman Creek to Speed Gap

The Bartram continues a short distance to where it crosses Dicks Creek. As of this writing, the bridge is out, having been destroyed during heavy rains in 2020; the Forest Service is expected to replace it in 2024 with a longer and higher bridge built to accommodate what have become increasingly intense high rainfall events and storms. When the stream is at normal flow, the crossing is only a foot deep or less, and the stream's bottom is clearly visible. Always exercise caution when wading the stream or using downed trees to cross. There have been accidents here, with serious injuries occurring to hikers attempting to walk across on downed trees. Hiking sticks help greatly.

9.4 The Chattooga River Trail connects to the Bartram from the left at a Y intersection and is marked with a light green rectangle. This trail travels 10.6 miles to US 76, paralleling Section III of the Chattooga, with incredibly scenic views of the river and multiple camping opportunities. There are two bridges out on this section, so be prepared to rock hop or wade. Continue on the Bartram Trail for 0.1 mile until reaching Sandy Ford Road.

9.5 Reach Sandy Ford Road. Parking for this trailhead is a short distance north on Sandy Ford Road. To the left, the road continues down to the Chattooga River and another ancient ford.

SECTION *2*

Sandy Ford Road to Warwoman Dell

(9.3 MILES)

My road for a considerable time led me winding and turning about the steep rocky hills; the descent of some of which was very rough and troublesome, by means of fragments of rocks, slippery clay and talc; but after this I entered a spacious forest, the land having gradually acquired a more level surface; a pretty grassy vale appears on my right, through which my wandering path led me, close by the banks of a delightful creek, which sometimes falling over steps of rocks, glides gently with serpentine meanders through the meadows.

Cultural and Natural History

Sandy Ford is a shallow and ancient crossing of the Chattooga River approximately one mile to the south of where the Bartram Trail crosses Sandy Ford Road. The Sandy Ford section of the Chattooga is where two dugout canoes have been found, each dating to at least 200 years earlier; one was carbon dated to approximately 1760. Both canoes showed evidence of being carved with metal tools, indicating possible European construction—or Cherokee construction, since by then the Cherokees had access to such tools through trade. At a recent archeological dig at the Cowee Mound site, remains of iron ore were found, indicating that colonial traders living there in the 18th century were manufacturing iron tools and implements.

It is amazing that less than 100 years after Bartram passed through this then-wild landscape, there would be plans for a railroad to cross at this ancient ford. Clayton, GA, was envisioned by investors as an industrial hub, with rail lines closely following the ancient Native American trail system that intersected near the Cherokee village of Stekoe at a location known as The Dividings. Clayton has become a recreational hub instead, as the railroad was never completed due to the Civil War. However, remains of the effort to build the Blue Ridge Railroad, which would have connected Anderson, SC, to Knoxville, TN, and link it to the old Tallulah Falls Railroad, are scattered throughout this area. What we have now are state roads and highways that were built upon these ancient trails. Warwoman Road, US 441, Highway 28 to Highlands, Highway 76 toward Hiawassee and South Carolina, and many county roads all crisscross this landscape over an ancient network of precolonial trade and travel.

The western end of the half-finished Dicks Creek railroad tunnel is on private land, but stone abutments can be seen off Sandy Ford Road and Warwoman Creek, and part of the original railroad bed can be seen at Warwoman Dell. Although the rail line was never built, industrial logging made its way into the area following the Civil War; the logging companies were mainly northern industrial operations that introduced narrow gauge railroads, commercial skidders, and heavy equipment into the mountains, destroying streams with splash dams and sedimentation, transforming self-sufficiency into a wage economy, and degrading the landscape into a cutover wasteland that was subject to intense fires and erosion. The passage of the 1911 Weeks Act created a National Forest System for the eastern United States, and following its enactment the U.S. Forest Service began buying up hundreds of thousands of acres in the southern Appalachians from the very companies that had ravaged them. These lands were cheap during the Depression, and the Forest Service was often able to purchase them for as little as $3 an acre from these companies and from mountain families who were suffering greatly and desperate for cash. Many local men at this time were employed by the newly formed Civilian Conservation Corps (est. 1933) to reforest the forest areas they had once been employed to cut, and to build a new future for the region by restoring these lands with recreational campgrounds, roads, parks, and trails. It is not hard to imagine that had that early rail line been completed, this beautiful forest landscape, enjoyed by outdoor enthusiasts of all sorts, would be very different from the one you are walking through now.

Section Overview

Access: To reach the Sandy Ford trailhead, travel east on Warwoman Road from US 441 in Clayton for 5.8 miles and make a slight right onto Sandy Ford Road; after 0.1 mile make a sharper right to stay on Sandy Ford Road. The road is gravel, but it's fairly well maintained. Bear left across Warwoman Creek in 0.7 mile and continue on Sandy Ford Road for another 3.3 miles until reaching Dicks Creek and a ford across it. This crossing can be difficult during high water, and thus this route is not reliable access for low clearance vehicles. (In the past, parking was allowed at this remote crossing, but it is now posted private property, so parking here is not advised.) Cross the stream, and in 0.3 mile there is parking on both sides of the road. The trail is another 0.1 mile down the road. For access to Pool Creek Road and Bob Gap, travel east from Clayton on Warwoman Road, turn right onto Sandy Ford Road, and travel 2.3 miles to Pool Creek Road; the road is not marked very well, but it is clearly a road. Turn right onto Pool Creek Road and travel 0.9 mile to Bob Gap. Pool Creek Road continues for another 4.3 miles until reaching US 76.

Much of this section follows ridgeline, slowly gaining elevation until descending to Warwoman Dell. Rainy Mountain is one of the highlights, and though the detour includes climbing to the summit and scrambling down its western side a bit to a large rock outcrop and overlook, it is worth the effort. There is also good camping at the summit, just off the Bartram Trail. The forest is mostly a recovering hardwood forest with an understory of mountain laurel and rhododendron. There are some large shortleaf pines on this section, along with white pines, Virginia pines, and pitch pines.

9.5 Cross Sandy Ford Road (elevation 1,625 ft) and climb gradually into a mixed hardwood forest before reaching the summit of a small peak (1,800 ft) in 0.3 mile. The forest becomes dominated by white pines at the summit. Continue for 0.3 mile, paying attention to trail markers, before bearing right onto an old road at 10.1 miles. The trail will now follow the ridgeline, reaching the carved granite Bartram Trail marker for Speed Gap at 11.4 miles.

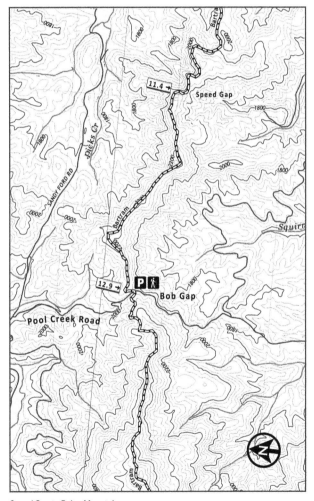

Speed Gap to Rainy Mountain

11.4 Follow the trail out of Speed Gap, where traces of illegal ATV trails remain on intersecting old roads, and then walk the spine of a narrow ridge. In winter there are great views to the north of Rabun Bald and Flat Top Mountains. You will now be looking across Warwoman Valley and will have attained an elevation of 2,160 feet. The trail begins to descend at 12.5 miles, reaching Bob Gap and Pool Creek Road at 12.9.

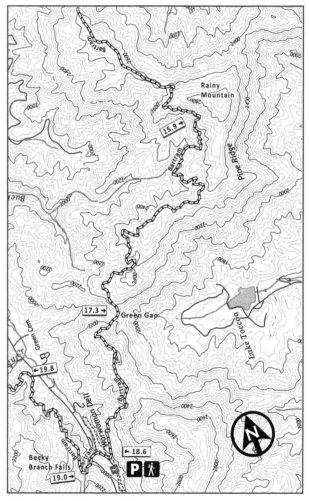

Rainy Mountain to Warwoman Dell

12.9 The trail crosses Pool Creek Road here and can be accessed by Sandy Ford Road. After you cross Pool Creek Road, climb around the north side of the ridge until reaching an old road, ascending to the ridgeline, and bearing right at the summit. The trail follows the ridgeline, passing through a campsite at 14.0 miles, where water can be found 500 steep feet down the southwest slope of the site. The elevation here is 2,700 feet.

14.7 Campsites with an intermittent spring can be found 500 feet down into the northwest cove. The trail climbs from here and bears right, leaving the road. There is another water source 0.2 mile north.

15.9 Past a side trail to Rainy Mountain, you will see a marked trail that leads to the summit and a good albeit overused camping area. Beyond the camping area, the trail steeply descends to a rock outcrop with excellent views to the west. The trail has historically been used and maintained by the Rainy Mountain Boy Scout Camp, which is visible from the overlook. If not making the trip to Rainy Mountain, continue on the Bartram, following the ridgeline and passing a campsite at 16.4 miles before arriving at an old road intersection at Green Gap at 17.3.

17.3 Note the large boulder on which is engraved *Bartram Trail, Green Gap, Warwoman Dell 1.3.* Continue north, crossing three wooden footbridges over seasonal streams and descending until reaching the gravel parking area at Warwoman Dell at 18.6 miles (elevation 1,950 ft). After arriving at the parking area, follow the road out to the right for 0.1 mile until reaching Becky Branch, where the trail turns left and leaves the road. Follow Becky Branch upstream for 0.1 mile before reaching Warwoman Road at 18.8.

Warwoman Dell to Wilson Gap

(8.5 MILES)

After passing through this meadow, the road led me over the bases of a ridge of hills, which as a bold promontory dividing the fields I had just passed, form expansive green lawns. On these towering hills appeared the ruins of the ancient famous town of Sticoe. Here was a vast Indian mount or tumulus and great terrace, on which stood the council house, with banks encompassing their circus; here were also old Peach and Plumb orchards, some of the trees appeared yet thriving and fruitful.

Cultural and Natural History

This section begins at Warwoman Dell Recreation Area, which the Civilian Conservation Corps (CCC) constructed in the late 1930s. The CCC built the covered structures that are still in use, along with trout runs, springhouses, and other features. Warwoman's name is derived from the Cherokee woman *Nanyehi*, or Nancy Ward, born circa 1738 in the Cherokee capital town of Chota in what is now southeastern Tennessee. Her mother was the sister of Attakullakulla, the Cherokee chief whom William Bartram encountered on his journey out of the Nantahala Mountains. Nanyehi was awarded the title of *Ghigau* or "Beloved Woman" by the Cherokee for her role in the 1755 Battle of Taliwa against the Muskogee Indians. Nanyehi picked up the gun dropped by her slain husband during the battle and led the Cher-

okee to victory, securing the north Georgia region for the Cherokee people. As Ghigau, she became the only female voting mem-
ber of the Cherokee General Council. She later married the Irish
trader Bryant Ward and took the name Nancy. Bryant Ward was
already married to a woman in South Carolina, however, and he
left Nancy after a short period and returned to his other family.
Nancy Ward went on to perform many important roles with the
Cherokee, such as helping to negotiate a peace agreement, the
Treaty of Hopewell, with representatives of the fledgling U.S.
government in 1785.

Another theory for the origin of the place name *Warwoman* is
that it comes from Nancy Morgan Hart, famous for her exploits
against loyalists in northeast Georgia during the Revolutionary
War. Hart had settled with her family in Georgia's upper Broad
River valley during the early 1770s. The accounts of her interesting life include variations on the story of a group of loyalist
soldiers who showed up at her home demanding food and bev-
erage. Hart agreed to host them and asked the group that they
place their guns against the wall. She slowly passed the guns out
the window to her husband as the soldiers continued to drink
before killing two of them with one of their own weapons. The
remainder of the group were hanged outside by her husband.

Evidence of the failed 19th-century Blue Ridge Railroad can
also be found at the Dell. Construction of the rail line had begun
prior to the Civil War, with numerous investors and schemes
that continued after the war. Had the railroad been completed,
Rabun County would have been a major connecting point between Charleston, Knoxville, and other southern cities, with the
likely result that the surrounding area would be much less rural
and remote.

This section of the trail also crosses the historically accepted route and ancient trade path on which Bartram traveled
by horseback, though the route proposed by cartographer Lamar Marshall (as discussed in section 1) is more likely. Bartram
is believed to have crossed the Chattooga at Earls Ford and then
proceeded up Warwoman Creek on an old trade path to Martin
Creek Falls, crossing over the Blue Ridge Mountains at Courthouse Gap. Hikers can pass by or take the side trail to Pinnacle
Knob, where Bartram is historically believed to have been when

describing a new species of magnolia he dubbed *Magnolia auriculata* (he called it "mountain magnolia" in subsequent writings). This species, with its large lobed leaves and smooth gray bark, was later named after the Scottish botanist John Fraser. Fraser learned of the species from the French botanist André Michaux, who explored the area in the 1780s and had learned of the species from Bartram. Fraser accompanied Michaux when the latter returned to Bartram's path into the mountains in 1787, but the two had somewhat of a falling-out, and Fraser proceeded on without Michaux. Fraser collected seeds and specimens and shipped them to England, where his friend and fellow botanist Thomas Walter assigned the name *Magnolia fraseri* to the species, with no credit to Bartram. Bartram, being Bartram, suffered this often with his descriptions, as he was without ego and was nonconfrontational about such matters.

It has generally been accepted that from this point Bartram crossed Courthouse Gap on an ancient trail and proceeded down to the destroyed and abandoned Cherokee village of Stekoe, near modern-day Clayton. On this section of his journey, he describes hundreds of acres of strawberries and expansive green lawns, the remains of Cherokee agriculture. In Stekoe, he describes stone piles in the old village, which he assumed marked the interred remains of Cherokee warriors killed in the earlier Creek wars. He also describes the mound of the village that was later razed for the modern-day town of Clayton. Stekoe was known as The Dividings, as numerous ancient trade paths intersected there. One of these led northward to Cowee, and another was a path to the northwest through the Hiwassee River valley and on to the Overhill Towns, Bartram's intended destination, which was near modern-day Loudon, Tennessee. Bartram had planned to meet a guide in the Cherokee village of Cowee who would lead him to the Overhill Towns, but the guide never showed, leading to Bartram's solo journey into the Nantahala Mountains along yet another ancient route.

Section Overview

Access: From US 441 in Clayton, travel east on Warwoman Road for 2.9 miles; just beyond the Forest Service sign on the right, turn right onto Warwoman Dell Lane. The parking area on the left upon entry is just a few feet from where the Bartram Trail heads up Becky Branch. Hikers going toward Sandy Ford can

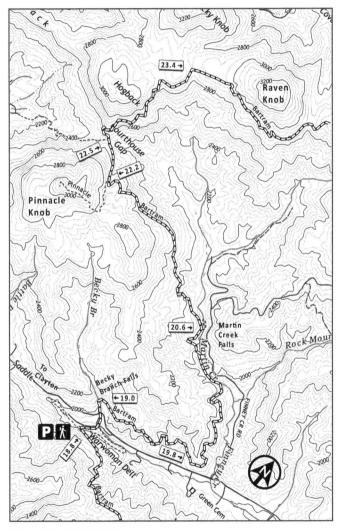

Warwoman Dell to Raven Knob

drive on to the parking area at the end of the road. There is a composting privy at the second parking area and a large pavilion with a fireplace, as well as an easy and short loop trail to a waterfall and an interpretive kiosk. The Bartram Trail departs this parking area on a set of steps to the south, and there is a stone marker just left of the privy.

18.8 After leaving the Warwoman parking area, the trail climbs up to Warwoman Road. Cross Warwoman Road with extreme caution and proceed toward Becky Branch Falls. You will see a state historical marker honoring Bartram where the trail crosses the road. This heavily traveled section is popular for day use due to its proximity to two waterfalls—Becky Branch and Martin Creek.

19.0 Reach Becky Branch Falls. The bridge is out but is scheduled to be replaced in 2024; the rock hop across the stream can be treacherous in high water but is not dangerous during average flow. Hikers wanting a brief loop hike from Warwoman Dell can rock hop across the branch and descend on the side trail to the right to get back to the parking area. If you continue on the Bartram for another half mile, the trail crosses a gated Forest Service road before descending to a small, unnamed tributary to Martin Creek. In the short distance between this road and the creek, the attentive hiker can see the rarest of mountain shrubs, mountain camellia, which Bartram discovered and described in his *Travels*. If you are hiking the Bartram Trail in June, look for the mountain camellia's spectacularly showy white flowers scattered on the trail.

19.8 The trail moves away from the noise of Warwoman Road and is soon winding its way above Martin Creek on an old roadbed, where the creek can be seen cascading down a narrow gorge toward its confluence with Warwoman Creek. The trail soon parallels the creek, requiring a rock hop across a small tributary at 20.6 miles.

20.6 Across Martin Creek is an overused dispersed camping and day-use area that is accessed via Finney Creek Road. You'll find more campsites along the trail just past this camping area, but be aware of dead hemlocks that could fall during high winds; by the time of this publication, they are likely to all be down. The trail turns right at the campsites and crosses Martin Creek on a footbridge. After you cross the bridge, turn left, and in 0.1 mile recross the creek on a footbridge to the left. This footbridge has an observation deck and offers an excellent view of the falls. Historians such as Frances Harper believe this is the "Falling Creek" that Bartram described in his journey through the area, though as mentioned earlier, others have posited that he traveled up to the Highlands Plateau and back along Overflow Creek. Regardless, it is a lovely place to enjoy a nice cool spray on a hot summer day and reflect on the area as Bartram would have seen it in May 1775.

Leaving the viewing platform, travel back downstream and make a sharp right turn at the camping area, after which you will begin ascending steeply uphill, crossing several small streams and moving away from Martin Creek along the ridgeline of Pinnacle Knob.

22.2 A green-blazed side trail to the west leaves the Bartram and gradually ascends a mile until reaching Pinnacle Knob, where Bartram describes *Magnolia auriculata*, or Fraser magnolia. Though he had encountered this plant on his way into the mountains, he is particularly struck by it here, christening the peak "mount Magnolia." The elevation here is 2,670 feet. The Bartram Trail follows an old road from here, descending to Courthouse Gap at 2,520 feet. Interestingly, in the present day no Fraser magnolias can be found along this trail or on the summit, which is populated primarily with gnarly old pitch pines but offers a spectacular view to the west. This once again lends credence to Marshall's proposition for the route Bartram actually traveled.

22.5 Courthouse Gap Trail heads down and west from Pinnacle Knob for 0.5 mile until reaching Courthouse Gap Road. For those wanting a shorter hike to the Pinnacle, this trail is much shorter and easier than hiking from Warwoman Dell. The total round trip from the Courthouse Gap trailhead on Courthouse Gap Road is 3.6 miles, with an elevation gain of approximately 1,000 feet. To access Courthouse Gap Trail, travel 0.7 mile north on US 441 from Warwoman Road in Clayton and turn right onto Pinnacle Drive. Follow Pinnacle Drive for 1.2 miles and turn left onto un-

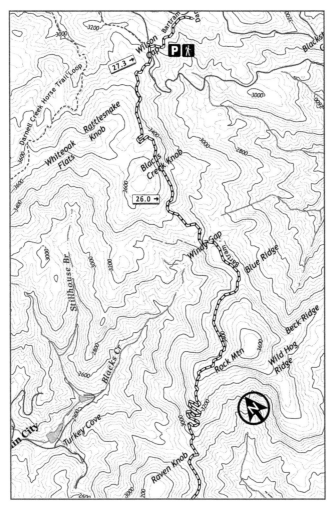

Raven Knob to Wilson Gap

paved Courthouse Gap Road. After 0.3 mile you will see a small parking area on the left. The trail is 250 feet up the road on the left, and there is no parking at the trailhead.

23.4 You will reach the Eastern Continental Divide as you skirt the south side of Raven Knob. Raven Knob reaches an elevation of 3,125 feet, and the trail passes below at 2,920 feet around the 23.8 mark. There is some camping at a small, intermittent stream just past this point, and there are more dry campsites along the way as the trail begins to follow the divide, skirting Rock Mountain and reaching Windy Gap at 26.0. You'll find another dry campsite at Windy Gap, along with a rock marker engraved *Bartram Trail* and *Windy Gap*.

26.0 The trail skirts Blacks Creek Knob (3,590 ft) and gradually descends to Wilson Gap (3,220 ft) at 27.3.

27.3 Wilson Gap is a large campsite with water 350 feet down the northwestern cove. Gated Forest Service road (FS) 155 is to the east of the site, and the Bartram Trail proceeds out of the gap to the northeast. FS 153 enters the gap from the north, which makes the site slightly less desirable due to potential intrusions from vehicles.

To access Wilson Gap, travel east on Warwoman Road from US 441 in Clayton for 6.2 miles and turn left onto Tuckaluge Creek Road. Tuckaluge Creek Road turns into FS 153, a gravel road. Follow FS 153 until it bears left and ends, staying straight onto FS 155A. At Walnut Creek Road/FS 155 (5.0 miles after turning onto Tuckaluge Creek Road), turn left and uphill, staying on FS 155A. The Bartram Trail crosses FS 155A at 1.3 miles from the hard left, and Wilson Gap is another 0.6 miles past that crossing. Both 153 and 155A are steep and rutted in places, and the road is not recommended for low clearance vehicles. High clearance four-wheel-drive vehicles are required to drive to Wilson Gap from the point where the Bartram crosses 155A.

Wilson Gap to Hale Ridge Road, Georgia / North Carolina Border

(9.2 MILES)

Presently after leaving these ruins, the vale and fields are divided by means of a spur of the mountains pushing forward; here likewise the road forked, the left hand path continued up the mountains to the Overhill towns; I followed the vale to the right hand, and soon began again to ascend the hills, riding several miles over very rough, stony land, yielding the like vegetable productions as heretofore; and descending again gradually, by a dubious winding path, leading into a narrow vale and lawn, through which rolled on before me a delightful brook, water of the Tanase.

Cultural and Natural History

This section of trail roughly parallels Bartram's journey into the Little Tennessee River Valley. Bartram proceeded down the valley after crossing the Eastern Continental Divide at modern-day Mountain City, GA, traveling north on an ancient trade path. Bartram describes his journey out of Stekoe and across the divide as being on a path of very rough and stony ground. Today that path is US 441, paved and four laned, and busy around the clock. He doesn't mention crossing the Eastern Continental Divide, which is interesting, as the location was known as Herbert's Savannah and was identified as such on mid-18th-century maps that Bartram likely would have seen. John Herbert traveled into the Little Tennessee River Valley while serving as Commissioner of Indian Affairs for South Carolina in the first part of the 18th century. Maps that show the savannah in the 18th century indicate that it was significant, and over 100 years later the U.S. Army Corps of Engineers (USACE) would describe it as one of the most significant depressions in the entire Blue Ridge; the USACE planned to build a canal across the savannah to connect the two watersheds that drained on either side of it. It held mythological significance as well, as the Cherokees believed that a particular spring draining into this unusual location produced enchanted water, and that anyone who drank the water would be captive to the area for seven years. Indian trader James Adair learned of the spring and this myth when passing through the area in 1755 and included an account of both in his *History of the American Indians*, published in London in 1775.

Water flowing into the savannah from the many springs in the mountains commingled in the large depression, which was likely flooded in part due to the large number of beavers that existed in the mountains at that time. The 19th-century travel writer Charles Lanman described the spring as a place "where the two great rivers 'shake hands,'" a description he ostensibly gathered from a Cherokee man in north Georgia. One of southern Appalachia's first women authors, Mary Noailles Murfree (1850-1922), included the spring as a central part of her short story "A Victor at Chungke," published in *Harper's Magazine* in March 1900.

Regardless, Bartram crossed the divide and headed into the upper Little Tennessee River Valley, where he observed abandoned farms and the ruins of Cherokee villages destroyed during two campaigns of the French and Indian War; he also took note of piles of stones along his route: "I observed on each side of the road many vast heaps of these stones, Indian graves undoubtedly." Interestingly, the upper valley is still agricultural, with numerous roadside farms dotting the landscape, beginning at Rabun Gap, GA, and continuing into Otto, NC.

This landscape will not be the one you experience as you ascend the Eastern Continental Divide to Rabun Bald, Georgia's second-highest mountain at 4,696 feet. However, at Rabun Bald you will look directly into the Little Tennessee River Valley to the west and see Scaly Mountain and the Fishhawk Range to the north. The Continental Divide runs southwest to northeast in its geography, spanning almost the entire eastern United States, and as you hike this section keep in mind that water on the eastern side of the mountain range ultimately flows to the Atlantic Ocean, while water on the western side flows into the Gulf of Mexico.

Rabun Bald sits within a 12,000-acre tract that was once owned by the lumberman Andrew Gennett. Gennett purchased this and other similarly sized tracts in Rabun County for eight dollars an acre in 1907 and subsequently logged a great deal of the Chattooga River watershed. He also owned thousands of acres elsewhere in the north Georgia and western North Carolina mountains and sold most of these cutover tracts to the U.S. Forest Service following the passage of the Weeks Act in 1911, which created an eastern National Forest System. Gennett was an avid journalist of his travels throughout the mountains, and his writings are full of interesting human interactions and logging tales. These were published under the title *Sound Wormy: Memoir of Andrew Gennett, Lumberman* (University of Georgia Press, 2007), thanks to the efforts of the book's editor, Nicole Hayler, who is also executive director of the Chattooga Conservancy.

Section Overview

Access: Access to Wilson Gap is described at the end of section 3, but there are three other access points for this section of the Bartram Trail. The first is the 1.4-mile-long **Alex Mountain Trail,** which begins in Sky Valley, GA, and connects to the Bartram Trail a half mile south of Rabun Bald. This trail is well maintained by Sky Valley residents and can be accessed by driving into the Sky Valley community via GA 246 out of Dillard. (The access point for the Alex Mountain Trail in Sky Valley is being changed to a new location currently, so check your favorite trail app for updates.) Most hikers wanting to climb Rabun Bald access this trail section at Beegum Gap. **To get to the Beegum Gap trailhead,** travel east on GA 246 from US 441 in Dillard for 4.2 miles and turn right onto Old Mud Creek Road.

Old Mud Creek Road becomes Bald Mountain Road in 0.4 mile. Travel along Bald Mountain Road for 2.6 miles and then turn right onto Kelsey Mountain Road. Parking is 0.3 mile ahead at the end of the road. Parking is limited and can be difficult on weekends and in the summer months. The summit of Rabun Bald is 1.6 miles from the parking area. **The Hale Ridge Road trailhead** is accessed by taking GA 246 east from US 441 in Dillard for 6.9 miles to the Scaly Mountain community (246 be-

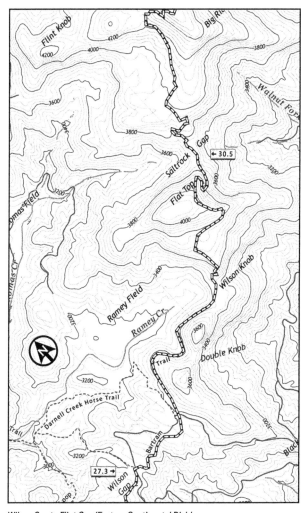

Wilson Gap to Flint Gap/Eastern Continental Divide

comes NC 106/Dillard Road after you cross into North Carolina a second time) and turning right onto Hale Ridge Road. Travel 2.1 miles on Hale Ridge Road and then bear left at Bald Mountain Road to stay on Hale Ridge Road. Continue for another mile and the trailhead will be on the right.

27.3 From Wilson Gap (3,220 ft), the trail winds its way up to FS 155, crossing it after 0.6 mile. You will see a Bartram Trail boulder at this point with *Bartram Trail* and *Rabun Bald 5* engraved on it. The trail gently begins winding its way around the west and northeast sides of Double Knob, Wilson Knob (3,417 ft), and Flat Top Mountain before reaching Saltrock Gap (3,700 ft) at 30.5. This section has numerous campsites, some with intermittent water, as well as small rock outcrops with good views. The water source for Saltrock Gap is 0.2 mile north.

30.5 Gradually ascend for 1.1 miles before reaching Flint Gap (4,300 ft) at 31.6. The Alex Mountain Trail leaves the Bartram Trail here and travels 1.3 miles to Sky Valley; local residents mark and maintain this unofficial trail. There are two great rock outcrops with views to the west and southwest on the Alex Mountain Trail. Ascend for another 0.7 mile until reaching the summit of Rabun Bald (4,696 ft) at 32.3. There is a decent, dry campsite 0.3 mile before the summit. The Civilian Conservation Corps built the old firetower at the summit in the 1930s under the supervision of Georgia's first Forest Service ranger, Roscoe Nicholson (known as "Ranger Nick"), and the structure remained in use until the 1970s, when a Youth Conservation Corps removed the enclosed observation tower and replaced it with the wooden platform it now has. This popular day-use area offers 360-degree views and can be crowded on beautiful fall weekends. Georgia's highest school, Bald Mountain School, operated at Rabun Bald in the early 1900s. It was a one-room log cabin that had 12 students and eight grades in 1914. Two boulders at the summit are engraved *Bartram Trail, Hale Ridge Road 4, Warwoman Dell 14* and *Three Forks Trail, Hale Ridge Road 3*. The Three Forks Trail leaves the summit of Rabun Bald to the northeast and is unmaintained.

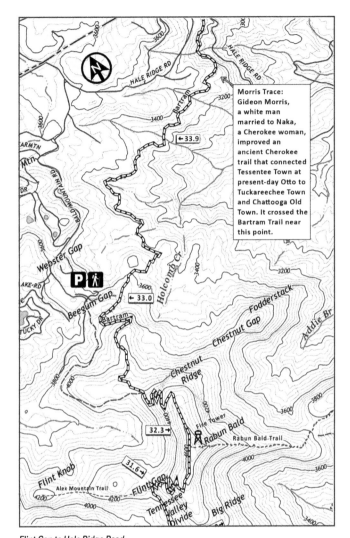

Morris Trace:
Gideon Morris,
a white man
married to Naka,
a Cherokee woman,
improved an
ancient Cherokee
trail that connected
Tessentee Town at
present-day Otto to
Tuckareechee Town
and Chattooga Old
Town. It crossed the
Bartram Trail near
this point.

Flint Gap to Hale Ridge Road

32.3 The Bartram Trail descends from Rabun Bald on an old jeep road that was built by Forest Service ranger Earl Parson in the 1940s but soon fell into disrepair. Poor drainage and design, along with heavy use, have led to severe erosion problems on the trail down to Beegum Gap, and rehabilitation and relocation efforts are planned for this section.

33.0 Reach the Y intersection where a short trail to the left leads to Beegum Gap and a parking area. There is a good water source 100 yards down the cove to the east. Bear right at the Y and continue on the Bartram for 0.9 miles on an old road before crossing another old road that leads to Beegum Gap on the left. Private property and a house are just 50 feet to the left.

33.9 There are numerous small streams and bridges for the next 2.6 miles until the Georgia / North Carolina border, with decent campsites to be found at 35.2 and 35.4, and great views to the east before the trail reaches the state line.

36.5 The trail reaches Hale Ridge Road. Turn right and walk 100 feet down the road to where the trail leaves the road on the left. There is an information kiosk with a map of the North Carolina segment of the Bartram Trail. This marks the end of the boulders engraved with destinations and mileage that characterize the Georgia segment of the Bartram.

PART II

North Carolina

Hale Ridge Road to Jones Gap

(10.8 MILES)

I continued several miles, pursuing my serpentine
path, through and over the meadows and green
fields, and crossing the river, which is here incredibly
increased in size, by the continual accession of
brooks flowing in from the hills on each side,
dividing their green turfy beds, forming them into
parterres, vistas and verdant swelling knolls, profusely
productive of flowers and fragrant strawberries,
their rich juice dying my horses feet and ancles.

Cultural and Natural History

This section represents the beginning of Bartram's journey into
the heart of the Middle Town Cherokees and "the great vale
of Cowe[e]," which he describes as having "one of the most
charming natural mountainous landscapes perhaps any where
to be seen." Bartram followed an ancient trade path to the capital of the Middle Town Cherokees, Cowee, far below this section
of the Bartram Trail, which ascends and traverses the Fishhawk
mountain range before descending into the Little Tennessee
River Valley near Otto, NC.

   As Bartram passed through this section of the upper Little
Tennessee River Valley, he described the destroyed towns and
agricultural remnants of the French and Indian War campaigns
fought here. The source of the conflict was the killing of Cher-

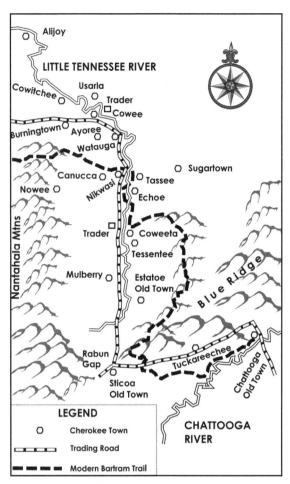

Bartram's route through Cherokee towns

okee warriors by Virginia frontiersmen in 1758 while the Cherokees were returning home from defending the Virginia frontier for the British. The Cherokees were obligated by their own justice system to enact vengeance and did so on nearby Carolina settlements instead of on the distant Virginia ones. Still, the Cherokees sought peace and sent the renowned Cherokee warrior Oconostota to Charlestown with a peace delegation in 1759. The delegation was refused by the South Carolina governor, William Henry Lyttelton, who sent them back to Fort Prince George with an escort of 1,300 militia and offered to exchange members of the delegation for the Cherokees guilty of killing the settlers.

Although this was an extremely difficult situation for the Cherokees based on their justice system, they nonetheless turned over three of their warriors, resulting in Oconostota and several others being released. However, Fort Prince George soldiers killed other members of the delegation, enraging the Cherokees and leading to further violence in the Overhill Towns and to two British military campaigns against the Cherokees in the Little Tennessee River Valley. The first, in 1760, was led by Colonel Archibald Montgomerie, who invaded Cherokee country with 1,650 soldiers and destroyed five of the Lower Town Cherokee villages. The Middle Town Cherokees were able to turn Montgomerie's forces back, but the following year, Lieutenant Colonel James Grant led a successful campaign against the Middle Towns, weakening the Cherokees beyond recovery. Grant's forces burned fifteen of the Middle Towns, destroyed 1,500 acres of crops, and drove 5,000 Cherokees into the mountains to starve.

Bartram's destination as he entered Cherokee country in May 1775 was the Overhill Towns near modern-day Loudon, TN, where the Cherokee warriors killed by Virginia frontiersmen in 1758 had been returning home to. Bartram's auspicious encounter with the Cherokee chief Attakullakulla as he traveled through the Nantahala Mountains possibly saved his life (more on that in section 11).

Section Overview

Access: Access to the Hale Ridge Road trailhead is outlined in section 4. This section of the Bartram has three other access points—Osage Overlook, Hickory Knut, and Jones Gap. **To reach Osage Overlook,** travel 8.5 miles on GA 246/NC 106 from US 441 in Dillard, GA. From Main Street in Highlands, travel south on NC 106, locally called the Dillard Road, for 5.7 miles. The roadside pulloff has ample parking and a Bartram Trail information kiosk. **To reach the Hickory Knut Gap Road access,** travel 4.0 miles south of Highlands on 106 and turn right onto Turtle Pond Road. In 0.3 mile, bear left onto Hickory Knut

Gap Road. The parking area for the Hickory Knut trailhead is 0.3 mile ahead on the right. From US 441 in Dillard, travel 10.2 miles on GA 246/NC 106 and turn left onto Turtle Pond Road. The Hickory Knut Trail is across the road, and it is 0.8 miles to the Bartram Trail. **To reach Jones Gap from Dillard,** turn left onto Turtle Pond Road and travel 3.3 miles to the intersection with Dendy Orchard Road. Turn left and travel 1.6 miles on Dendy Orchard before turning left at FS 4522. There is a Bartram Trail sign at this intersection. Travel 2.0 miles on FS 4522 until reaching the road's end and Jones Gap. **To reach Jones Gap from Highlands,** take US 64W/28N from Dillard Road/106 for 4.2 miles and turn left onto Turtle Pond Road. Follow Turtle Pond Road for 1.1 miles to Dendy Orchard Road, then turn right and travel 1.6 miles on Dendy Orchard Road before turning left onto FS 4522. **To reach Jones Gap from Franklin,** follow NC 28S from East Main Street in downtown Franklin for 11.0 miles and turn right onto Gold Mine Road; the drive up 28 takes you through the spectacular Cullasaja Gorge. After turning onto Gold Mine Road, travel 0.8 mile and then turn left onto Dendy Orchard Road. Follow Dendy Orchard Road for 2.3 miles until reaching FS 4522. Turn right and travel 2.0 miles to Jones Gap.

The Bartram Trail crosses Hale Ridge Road at the Georgia / North Carolina border and then meanders through the headwaters of Overflow Creek for the next several miles. Overflow Creek descends rapidly from this area to its confluence with Holcomb and Big Creeks at the stunning location known as Three Forks on the upper West Fork of the Chattooga River. You are now on the Atlantic side of the Eastern Continental Divide and will be until ascending Scaly Mountain, when the trail enters the Little Tennessee Drainage for the remainder of its length. For 3.7 miles, to Osage Overlook and NC 106, the trail travels through the Overflow Wilderness Study Area, designated as such by Congress in 1984, when North Carolina's last Wilderness Act was passed. The ambiguous status of such a designation has left the area in limbo for 30 years, though it is protected as part of the Forest Service's roadless inventory, which means that it cannot be commercially logged or have new roads built through it.

For its duration, the trail in this section is in an ericaceous forest, a forest type dominated by mountain laurel and rhododendron; various species of blueberry, huckleberry, and barberry; and sourwood, pine, and oak trees. The trail also travels through 300 acres of old-growth forest, where large chestnut oaks and shortleaf pines dominate the surrounding forest. Water is abundant here, and there are a few good campsites. Rock outcrops appear along the trail as it approaches Osage Overlook,

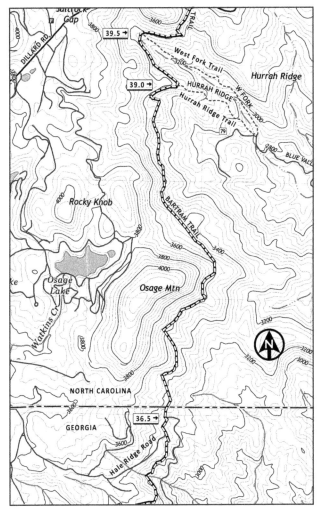

Hale Ridge Road to West Fork Trail

and one of the westernmost populations of the crevice-dwelling green salamander has been found along this section. There are also two options for loop hikes. The Puc Puggy Trail leaves the Bartram near the Osage Overlook parking area and rejoins it after 0.8 mile. There are also the West Fork and Hurrah Ridge Trails, which can be accessed most readily from Osage Overlook; you can make a loop by following either trail down to the Forest Service road and Overflow Creek and returning to the Bartram by the other trail. After leaving Osage Overlook and crossing NC 106, the trail climbs steeply at times to the summit of Scaly Mountain, one of many outstanding views along the North Carolina portion of the Bartram Trail.

36.5 From Hale Ridge Road, make a gentle climb into a mixed hardwood forest, skirting Osage Mountain on its southeast side, and then hike the next 2.4 miles on a well-contoured trail with multiple stream crossings on footbridges and rock hops. This segment offers occasional views of Rabun Bald to the south and of Scaly Mountain to the north.

39.0 Reach the Hurrah Ridge Trail intersection on the right. Hurrah Ridge Trail travels 0.6 miles to the end of FS 79 (Blue Valley Road). One hundred feet down the road is the West Fork Trail, which connects to the Bartram Trail at mile 39.5.

39.5 The West Fork Trail extends 0.9 miles to the right until its intersection with FS 79. Continue on the Bartram Trail to 39.7.

39.7 The Bartram intersects here with the Puc Puggy Trail, an alternative route to Osage Overlook. Old-growth shortleaf pines, chestnut oaks, and white pines can be seen on this trail. See the section on day hikes for more info. Or continue on Bartram Trail for 0.4 mile to Osage Overlook.

40.1 After reaching the Osage Overlook parking area, carefully cross NC 106 to the stairs climbing away from the road. From here the trail ascends—steeply at times, and occasionally gradually—through a mixed hardwood forest, climbing steadily to the intersection with the Hickory Knut trailhead at 41.5. There is signage at this intersection. The Hickory Knut Trail is 0.8 mile to the parking area on Hickory Knut Gap Road. See the section on day hikes for more info.

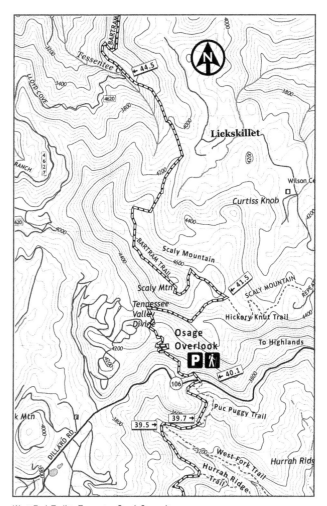

West Fork Trail to Tessentee Creek Campsite

41.5 The trail bears left toward Scaly Mountain for 0.5 mile, with occasional openings on the spine of the mountain, before reaching its summit at 4,804 feet. Here is one of the many great views of the upper Little Tennessee River Valley that will characterize the Bartram Trail on the way to the summit of Wayah Bald. Across the valley, you can see the Nantahala mountain range, which the Bartram Trail will climb on its route from Franklin. The Appalachian Trail lies on the ridgeline of the Nantahala Range, coming out of Georgia in the Southern Nantahala Wilderness and winding its way to its intersection with the Bartram at Wayah and Cheoah Balds to the north.

Scaly Mountain is a geological wonder. Its strange pock-marked features are due to an overthrust sheet that occurred here when Africa collided with the eastern portion of North America over 300 million years ago. This overthrust mass is composed of metamorphic layers from an even older period that eroded and then were deposited in layers that extended down to the earth's mantle. Heat and pressure produced layers of met-amorphic rock called *gneiss* and *schist*. Water draining across gneiss often follows little cracks. Some of the softer spots along the cracks begin to develop into small depressions. When it rains, these depressions become filled with humic acids and car-bonic acids from decaying organic matter and rain. Chemical breakdown furthers the depressions, forming what appears to be little animal hoof tracks. The trail descends from here through other outcrops with views, with mountain ash (rare for this area) growing on the northern slope, before entering dense rhododen-dron and mountain laurel and winding its way down to Tessen-tee Campsite at mile 44.5.

44.5 Tessentee Creek Campsite lies on an old Forest Service road that is gated and mostly unmaintained other than by Bar-tram Trail maintainers who occasionally access and clear the road to work on the trail. The campsite has a firepit and lantern pole and an excellent water source: upper Tessentee Creek. For thru-hikers, this is a good place to load up on water, as there isn't another reliable water source until the trail reaches Whiterock Mountain. The trail follows the road to the north from here for 0.2 mile before making a hard right away from the road on a set of log steps. The trail now climbs toward Hickory Gap, ascending through a recovering cutover forest until reaching a rock outcrop in 0.5 mile. Climb up and around the rock outcrop on the west side of Peggy Knob and descend on steep switchbacks for a short distance until climbing again toward Hickory Gap.

45.8 Cross a small ridge and head northeast around Peggy Knob. The forest begins to appear much older past this point, with some of the largest trees on the trail between here and Hick-ory Gap. Large chestnut oaks and northern red oaks can be seen

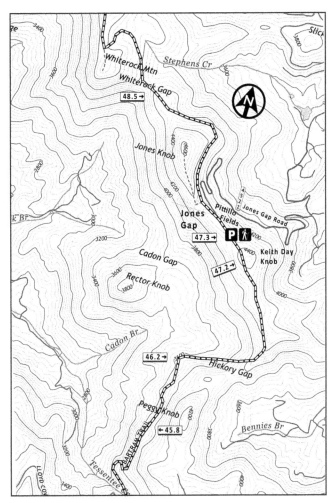

Tessentee Creek Campsite to Whiterock Mountain

along the trail; this small patch of remaining old-growth forest is testimony to what uncut rich cove forests looked like before the era of industrial logging.

46.2 Reach an old road and bear right, going up briefly and then making a left off the road. There is a small sign that may be missed if you are not looking for the left turn; missing the turn will take you up to a private driveway after 100 yards, in which case you will need to turn around and go back. Climb along the ridgeline of the Fishhawk mountain range for the next 0.6 mile to an outstanding rock outcrop with views to the south and southeast. Travel north from here until reaching the summit of Keith Day Knob at 47.2. Keith Day was an extremely dedicated trailbuilder and maintainer with the Bartram Trail Society for many years before his passing. From here, descend through a wildlife opening, which can be dense in spring and summer until volunteers mow the trail opening. Between the opening and Jones Gap is one of the richest locations for wildflowers in the area. In the spring you'll see a carpet of trillium and many other rich forest species.

47.3 Reach Jones Gap. A large parking area and an information kiosk for the trail are here.

Jones Gap to Hickory Knoll Road

(9.6 MILES)

My winding path now leads me again over the green fields into the meadows, sometimes visiting the decorated banks of the river, as it meanders through the meadows, or boldly sweeps along the bases of the mountains, its surface receiving the images reflected from the flowery banks above.

Thus was my agreeable progress for about fifteen miles, since I came upon the sources of the Tanase, at the head of this charming vale: in the evening espying a human habitation at the foot of the sloping green hills, beneath lofty forests of the mountains on the left hand, and at the same time observed a man crossing the river from the opposite shore in a canoe and coming towards me, I waited his approach, who hailing me, I answered I was for Cowe[e]; he intreated me very civilly to call at his house, adding that he would presently come to me.

Cultural and Natural History

The passage above describes Bartram's travels into the settled area of the Little Tennessee River Valley, south of modern-day Franklin and what was then the Cherokee village of Nikwasi, not far from the Cherokee village of Echoe to the north, and in the vicinity of modern-day Otto, NC. Views of this area are abundant on this section of trail, most notably from Whiterock Mountain. The trader Bartram encountered in this passage kept a

trading house and a stock of cattle and was married to a Cherokee woman, who served Bartram cream and strawberries. Bartram spent the night and enjoyed a breakfast of smoked venison,
excellent butter and cheese, and corn cakes before resuming his
travels. He describes the trade path as well beaten and spacious
but still difficult to follow due to the number of paths that came
into it from other villages spread throughout the mountains. By
this time, the Cherokee Nation had been reduced from its for-
mer greatness through wars and treaties, but there were numerous villages to the west across the Nantahala Mountains within
the Valley River watershed and east over the Cowee Mountains in the Tuckaseegee River Valley. A 1727 map by John Herbert showed his estimate of almost 10,000 people living in these
three river valleys. This was, of course, before the French and
Indian War campaigns, which reduced the population and destroyed villages that had not recovered by the time of Bartram's
visit to Cherokee country.

This section is characterized by some of the most outstanding views on the Bartram Trail, particularly for hikers making
the trek in winter, as the trail follows the spine of the Fishhawk
Range, providing incredible views for most of its duration. The
term *fish hawk* was historically used to describe the majestic os-
prey, which, after decades of absence from the area due to DDT,
is again a commonly seen bird on the Little Tennessee River. On
the east side of the Fishhawk Range, water drains into the Cullasaja River, a major tributary of the Little Tennessee River. Cullasaja was a Cherokee village so named for the honey locust
trees that were propagated there for the sweet pulp that could
be harvested from their distinctive autumn seed pods. Honey locust is native to central North America and is one of many species introduced by the Cherokees for food or medicinal reasons.
Concentrations of honey locust throughout the Little Tennessee River Valley generally indicate old Cherokee village sites or
farmsteads.

The west side of the Fishhawk Range is characterized by
large rock outcrops, with Whiterock Mountain being the largest. These are interesting botanical areas, dominated by eastern
redcedar (*Juniperus virginiana*) and many other species that are
uncommon in the southern Blue Ridge Mountains. Botanists of-

ten refer to these outcrops as "montane cedar glades," and hikers of this section will experience such a glade firsthand as they descend through the edge of the Pinnacle. A small population of feral goats were living within these outcrops several years ago, but they have not been seen in recent years.

Section Overview

Access: Jones Gap access is detailed in section 5. The only other road access point to this section is at its terminus at Hickory Knoll Road. The Hickory Knoll Road trailhead is reached by traveling north on US 441 from Bettys Creek Road in Dillard for 6.2 miles and turning right onto Tessentee Road in Otto, NC. Travel 1.1 miles on Tessentee Road and turn left onto Hickory Knoll Road. In 1.2 miles the parking area is on the left. The trail is directly across the road. This tract is owned by Mainspring Conservation Trust and managed by the Wildlife Resources Commission.

47.3 From Jones Gap (4,360 ft), walk around the Forest Service gate and proceed uphill until reaching a wildlife opening. The trail through this opening is mowed by the Blue Ridge Bartram Trail Conservancy but can grow quite dense between mowings. The apple tree here produces decent fruit in the fall. Bear right at the end of the opening, staying on the Bartram. Straight ahead is Jones Knob, which has an outstanding view of Tessentee Valley and Whiterock Mountain. The trail descends here a bit, following the east flank of Jones Knob through rhododendron and large chestnut oaks. You will also see the occasional American chestnut along this section. Look for the plant and tree identification markers placed at various locations by the trail conservancy in collaboration with the Highlands Garden Club. This section is rocky in places and can be treacherous when wet.

48.5 A short trail to the left leads to a large rock outcrop with views of Whiterock Mountain, the Nantahala Mountains, and the Tessentee and Little Tennessee River Valleys. Note the eastern redcedars at the outcrop; this is a species that dominates outcrops on the Fishhawk Range, along with other unusual species unique to these outcrops. Back on the Bartram, proceed downhill 0.1 mile until reaching Whiterock Gap at 4,130 feet. There is a small campsite here and water down the eastern cover. Begin your climb up to the trailhead for Whiterock Mountain. To your east is the Cullasaja River Valley, with its rugged gorge and numerous waterfalls.

49.0 The small sign for water here refers to an excellent high-elevation spring to the right of the trail. This is the last chance for water until near the section's end. In 0.1 mile the blue-blazed

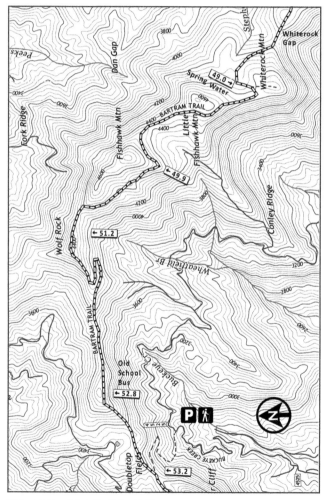

Whiterock Mountain to Doubletop Fields

trail for Whiterock Mountain bears left from the Bartram. It's a quarter mile to the large, exposed rock face, and well worth the extra trip to see the outstanding views and natural features. Continuing on the Bartram, climb Little Fishhawk Mountain (4,650 ft) and descend to the gap between Little Fishhawk and Fishhawk Mountain at 49.9, where you'll find a dry campsite.

49.9 Leave the gap and begin skirting the west side of Fishhawk Mountain, and in 0.2 mile there is a short (0.2 mile) side trail to the summit. It's a significant detour if you are hiking the length of this section in one day, much like climbing up Whiterock, but if you have the energy and time, it affords a rare view to the east from this elevation on the Fishhawk Range. The trail now descends from Fishhawk Mountain over the next 0.9 mile before ascending 0.2 mile to Wolf Rock Knob (4,450 ft) at 51.2.

51.2 For the next 1.6 miles, the trail, narrow and rocky at times, follows the ridgeline, passing the Wolf Rock Overlook before reaching the old school bus at 52.8. There is a dry campsite at 51.9 (3,900 ft).

52.8 Everyone wants to know the story of the old school bus. According to a reliable local source, the bus housed migrants working at a nearby orchard some years ago. Remnants of the orchard can be seen on private land to the north of the bus, which has also served as a hunter's cabin. The trail continues past the bus on the left, descending below the bus before making a near U-turn to the left. It's very easy to miss the left and go straight, so look for the yellow blazes. The trail passes through a small rock outcrop and follows the ridgeline until reaching Doubletop Gap and the junction with the Buckeye Creek Trail at 53.2.

53.2 It is 2.3 miles down the blue-blazed Buckeye Creek Trail to the trailhead at the end of Buckeye Branch Road. To reach this trailhead, head east on Tessentee Road from US 441 in Otto, NC, and after 3.3 miles turn left onto Buckeye Branch Road. Follow Buckeye Branch Road for 0.5 mile to a small parking area at road's end. It is 3.7 miles to Hickory Knoll Road from where Buckeye Creek Trail connects to the Bartram Trail.

For the next mile of the Bartram, travel along the ridgeline on the southeast side of Cedar Cliff, intersecting an old road at 53.9 and passing the only campsite before Hickory Knoll Road. There is a small spring 0.2 mile before reaching the campsite.

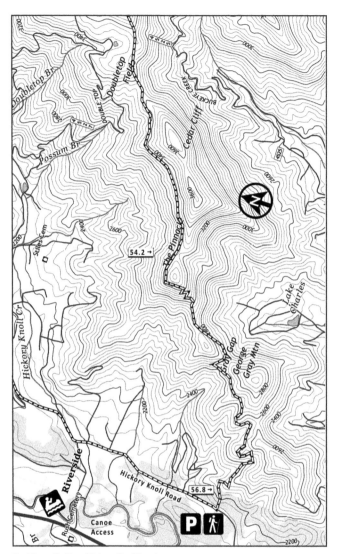

Doubletop Fields to Hickory Knoll Road

54.2 Reach the Pinnacle (not to be confused with Pinnacle Knob on the Georgia portion of the trail) and begin descending through a cedar glade, with an open rock outcrop on the east side of the trail, to a dry west-facing slope with mountain laurel. A cedar glade is an unusual plant community, and many species are found here that are rare elsewhere in Appalachia.

56.8 You will descend a long section of rock steps before reaching a kiosk along a private driveway. In the past the trail continued down the driveway, but now it goes left at the kiosk and through the forest until reaching the Hickory Knoll parking area after 0.1 mile. This 60-acre tract is owned by Mainspring Conservation Trust, and camping may be permitted if you notify the trust ahead of time. There is an information kiosk at the parking area and trailhead.

SECTION 7

Hickory Knoll Road
to Wallace Branch

(15.2 MILES BY ROAD/GREENWAY
OR 14.0 MILES BY RIVER/ROAD)

Next morning after breakfasting on excellent coffee,
relished with bucanned venison, hot corn cakes,
excellent butter and cheese, set forwards again for
Cowe[e], which was about fifteen miles distance,
keeping the trading path which coursed through the
low lands between the hills and the river, now spacious
and well beaten by travellers, but somewhat intricate
to a stranger, from the frequent collateral roads falling
into it from villages or towns over the hills: after riding
about four miles, mostly through fields and plantations,
the soil incredibly fertile, arrived at the town of Echoe,
consisting of many good houses, well inhabited; I passed
through and continued three miles farther to Nucasse,
and three miles more brought me to Whatoga: riding
through this large town, the road carried me winding
about through their little plantations of Corn, Beans,
&c. up to the council-house, which was a very large
dome or rotunda, situated on the top of an ancient
artificial mount, and here my road terminated.

Cultural and Natural History

When Bartram left the trader's cabin somewhere near modern-
day Otto, he was traveling into a more settled section of the valley, despite it having been destroyed fifteen years earlier in the
French and Indian War. He describes a well-traveled and agricultural landscape that has continued to this day—albeit full of

66

modern highways now, all of them built atop those old trails—with small but industrial agriculture operations throughout the valley. The valley was settled and farmed for more than 1,000 years before Bartram's arrival, crisscrossed with trails between villages and layered with a dense Cherokee cosmology that Bartram no doubt felt as he made his way toward Cowee. He makes little mention of reaching "Nucasse," or Nikwasi Mound (modern-day Franklin), though historically it was the gateway town to Cowee and the abode of the Nunehi, small Cherokee warriors who lived within the mound. Nikwasi—or Noquisiyi, as it was (and still is) called by the Cherokee prior to anglicization of the word—was one of the many spiritual, diplomatic, and ceremonial centers of the Cherokee people before their removal, and it only recently has been returned to Cherokee ownership.

Nikwasi means "star place," which may relate to the high concentrations of mica in the surrounding mountains, a mineral that the Cherokee used ceremonially and traded far and wide. Mica traded during this era has been found in cultural sites as far away as the upper Ohio River Valley. The town was destroyed during the French and Indian War, and the council house that sat atop the mound was used as a field hospital for British soldiers. American revolutionaries destroyed the town again the year after Bartram passed by, and it never recovered. Yet today the Cherokee, along with partners in the nonprofit Nikwasi Initiative and Mainspring Conservation Trust, are reacquiring these ancient town sites, including the Nikwasi, Watauga, Cowee, and Kituwah Mounds.

Bartram continued past Nikwasi to Watauga Town a few miles north of Franklin, where he describes a council house on a mound, and fields of beans and corn that he had to meander his horse through until reaching a standstill due to his fear of trampling the crops. He was greeted by the chief of Watauga, who welcomed him heartily and prepared him food. Bartram's visit here was not long, but it is a significant entry in his journal. He remarks on the respect that he received, but also on his own respect for the Cherokee people and their customs:

> During my continuance here, about half an hour, I experienced the most perfect and agreeable hospitality conferred on me by these happy people; I mean happy in their dispositions, in their

apprehensions of rectitude with regard to our social or moral conduct: O divine simplicity and truth, friendship without fallacy or guile, hospitality disinterested, native, undefiled, unmodified by artificial refinements.

Bartram describes a ceremonial smoking of tobacco with the chief, which was accomplished with a four-foot-long pipe adorned with snake skins and feathers, and a bright conversation with him about the royal superintendent of Indian affairs John Stuart, who was respected by the Cherokees for his honesty. The chief then had his sons feed corn to Bartram's horse—a sign of great honor and respect that was reserved for those whom the Cherokees held in the highest esteem. The chief then showed Bartram the path to Cowee and accompanied him for two of the five miles to the town. At noon Bartram arrived in Cowee, the diplomatic capital of the Middle Town Cherokees, describing its beauty along with the respect and hospitality with which he was received.

Use your imagination as you travel this section of the landscape, envisioning not only the past but also the future. Key acquisitions by the Eastern Band of Cherokee Indians, Mainspring Conservation Trust, the NC Wildlife Resources Commission, Macon County, the town of Franklin, Nikwasi Initiative, and the Blue Ridge Bartram Trail Conservancy are stitching the landscape together into a world-class cultural heritage corridor that will protect important cultural and sacred sites, as well as the high biodiversity of the Little Tennessee River watershed.

Section Overview

Though most hikers naturally avoid road walks, many of the thru-hikers traversing the length of the Bartram Trail will walk the 15.2 miles between Hickory Knoll Road and Wallace Branch so that they can say they have walked the entire trail. If you are a thru-hiker or section hiker who wants to say they have walked the entire trail from beginning to end, walk or paddle this section! The Bartram Trail was rerouted in 2023, eliminating the need to cross US 441 and US 64. Though this trail section is a few miles longer than the old route, it now travels through the Macon County Recreation Park (where showers and bathrooms are available), then onto the Little Tennessee River Greenway, and from there through downtown Franklin. This new route is much safer and more enjoyable and provides opportunities for solitude and rural scenery. The following section describes both the road/greenway option and the paddling option. Each offers a rewarding experience and should be considered. You will be gratified by the historical context, the rural landscape, and the satisfaction of having traveled every mile of the trail.

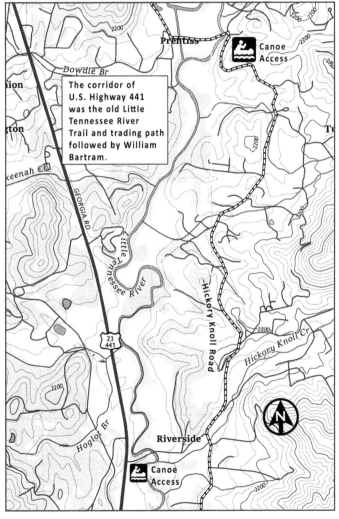

The corridor of U.S. Highway 441 was the old Little Tennessee River Trail and trading path followed by William Bartram.

Hickory Knoll Road to Prentiss Bridge

Access: To access the Hickory Knoll trailhead from Phillips Street in downtown Franklin, travel south on US 441 toward Clayton for 7.0 miles and turn left onto Riverside Road. Travel 0.5 mile on Riverside Road and turn right onto Hickory Knoll Road. The trailhead and parking area are 0.9 mile ahead on the right. This is a well-maintained lot with an information kiosk. The trail is directly across the road from the parking area.

ROAD/GREENWAY OPTION

Hickory Knoll Parking/Trailhead to Lazy Hiker Brewing: Travel 1.4 miles north on Hickory Knoll Road until reaching Clarks Chapel Road. Bear left onto Clarks Chapel Road and follow it for 2.1 miles. Turn left onto Prentiss Bridge Road, cross the Little Tennessee River, and continue for 0.3 mile to Wide Horizon Drive. Take a right at Wide Horizon Drive and follow it for 3.1 miles, turning right into the Macon County Fairgrounds. From the fairgrounds parking area, cross Cartoogechaye Creek on a footbridge, then turn left into the Macon County Recreation Park and parallel Cartoogechaye Creek upstream, skirting the ball fields until reaching a small gravel parking area at 0.3 mile. Follow the road uphill 0.1 mile from the parking area until reaching the park entrance. Turn right onto Allman Drive and follow it 0.1 mile until it dead-ends. From here, proceed straight onto the town of Franklin's gravel right-of-way, walking along the edge of a private field for 0.1 mile before turning left onto town property that will soon become part of the Little Tennessee River Greenway. The trail is mowed and blazed here and roughly parallels Cartoogechaye Creek for 0.4 mile until it reaches the Little Tennessee River Greenway. Follow the greenway for 3.1 miles until it crosses under Main Street, then turn left at Big Bear Shelter and onto Main Street. The trail continues west on Main Street through downtown Franklin to Lazy Hiker Brewing at 0.9 mile. Lazy Hiker is a great place to stop at for a visit.

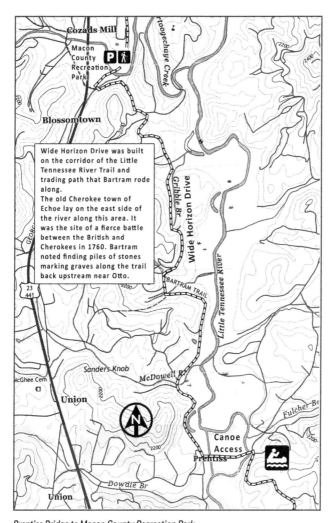

Wide Horizon Drive was built on the corridor of the Little Tennessee River Trail and trading path that Bartram rode along.

The old Cherokee town of Echoe lay on the east side of the river along this area. It was the site of a fierce battle between the British and Cherokees in 1760. Bartram noted finding piles of stones marking graves along the trail back upstream near Otto.

Prentiss Bridge to Macon County Recreation Park

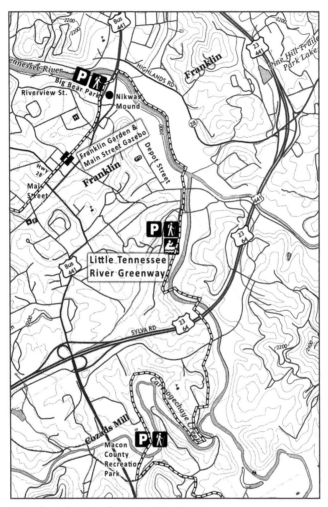

Macon County Recreation Park to Lazy Hiker Brewing

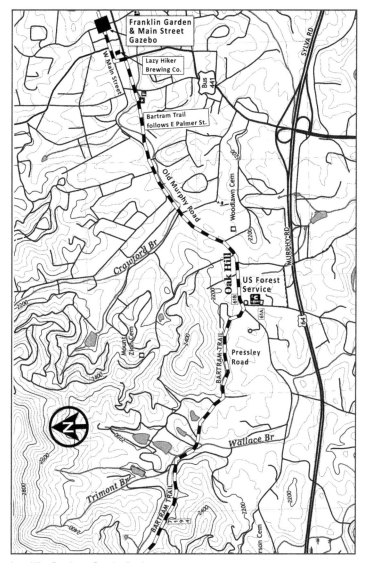

Lazy Hiker Brewing to Pressley Road

Lazy Hiker Brewing to Wallace Branch Trailhead: From Lazy Hiker, walk west on West Main Street for 0.2 mile and turn left at Commerce Street. In 378 feet turn right onto West Palmer Street, which will turn into Old Murphy Road in 0.7 mile. Continue on Old Murphy Road for 0.7 mile and turn right on Pressley Road. Follow Pressley Road for 1.0 mile until bearing right on Ray Cove Road. The road dead-ends at the trailhead in 0.7 mile. There is camping not far up the trail from the road's end. Camping at the Wallace Branch trailhead is not advised.

KAYAKING OR CANOEING OPTION

There are two options for boating after leaving the Hickory Knoll trailhead. From the Hickory Knoll parking area, a trail departs westward through an old field, extending 0.3 mile to the Little Tennessee River. There is no developed access to the river at this spot, which can be overgrown and unmaintained, but a kayak or canoe can be launched without too much difficulty. The Riverside Road boat launch is 1.2 miles from where the Bartram Trail exits the parking area at Hickory Knoll Road. It's roughly a 9-mile paddle from Hickory Knoll or an 8-mile paddle from the Riverside Road launch to the Tassee Shelter takeout on the Little Tennessee River Greenway, with the only possible problems being blowdowns, which must be portaged over or around. This is a low gradient section of the Little Tennessee River, and during dry weather it can be shallow, requiring a bit of dragging. It is a wonderful way to accomplish the entire trail, however, and closely follows Bartram's actual route through the valley. From the takeout at Tassee Shelter, walk up Depot Street to Main Street and turn left, traveling through downtown Franklin and continuing on the route described in the road/greenway option. Alarka Expeditions is a local guide and outfitter that can arrange kayak rentals, shuttles, and more.

Wallace Branch to Wayah Bald

(10.8 MILES)

I began again to ascend the Jore mountains, which
I at length accomplished, and rested on the most
elevated peak; from whence I beheld with rapture
and astonishment, a sublimely awful scene of power
and magnificence, a world of mountains piled upon
mountains. Having contemplated this amazing
prospect of grandeur, I descended the pinnacles, and
again falling into the trading path, continued gently
descending through a grassy plain, scatteringly planted
with large trees, and at a distance surrounded with
high forests, I was on this elevated region sensible
of an alteration in the air, from warm to cold, and
found that vegetation was here greatly behind, in
plants of the same kind of the country below.

Cultural and Natural History

Bartram arrived in Cowee to meet a guide to take him to the
Overhill Towns, near modern-day Loudon, TN. The guide never
showed, allowing Bartram to explore the surrounding area and
to provide us with the only description we have of Cowee Town
and Cherokee people during this period. It was May 1775, and
just a little over a year later Cowee and all the surrounding
Cherokee villages would be brutally destroyed by Rutherford's
troops in one of the early campaigns of the American Revolution. Bartram's encounters with southern Indians and his de-

scriptions of their villages and customs is one of the most important resources for that era of American history. Bartram was a radical for his time and argued for the equality of and respect for Native Americans, which was a main reason his book was not well received by his fellow citizens when it was published in 1791. It is worth quoting Bartram on Native American equality: "*Their ideas, with respect to the duties, and conduct of individuals, to their superiors, coincide with those of the most perfect government on earth. Are these people not worthy of our friendship? Are they not worthy of our care?... Who has a stronger claim to this country than the Indians? If priority of possession gives the best right, then surely they have it?*" These were radical views for the 18th century, and ones not shared by his father, John Bartram, whose own father—William's grandfather—had been killed by Indians on the Cape Fear River in the early 18th century.

While waiting on his guide, Bartram explored the Cowee mountain range across the valley from the Nantahala Mountains with a trader by the name of Patrick Galahan. Eventually Bartram decided to pursue his journey to the Overhill settlements alone. There were numerous trade paths across the Nantahala Mountains, but the main path out of Cowee to the Overhill Towns was across Burningtown Gap, where the Appalachian Trail now crosses. Galahan accompanied Bartram part of the way up the Nantahalas, taking him through the Cherokee village of Jore, now the location of the Macon County Airport. Bartram describes a grove of yaupon holly growing there, a coastal species that the Cherokees grew for ceremonial reasons. Our only native plant to contain caffeine, it was used as an emetic by all the southern Indians.

As he was climbing the Nantahalas, which were then called the Jore Mountains, Bartram began to reflect on his life and priorities, comparing himself to Nebuchadnezzar—"expelled from the society of men, and constrained to roam in the mountains and wilderness, there to herd and feed with the wild beasts of the forest." He startled a young Cherokee man hunting, but they were soon exchanging handshakes and smiles, and Bartram left his new acquaintance with some choice tobacco. Bartram returned to his gloomy state of mind and proceeded up to Burningtown Gap, from where he then climbed south to Wayah Bald on an ancient path that is now the Appalachian Trail. Here he made an important observation that Charles Darwin would later reference when considering the distribution of species. Bartram noted species that were identical yet isolated from one another by elevation and temperature and how their bloom times varied based on these factors. He had also observed this phenomenon earlier when traveling into the Oconee Mountains, approaching the Blue Ridge. He described a very rich forest in the Nantahala Mountains that was populated with ash, various species of oak, basswood, cucumber tree, elm, viburnum, Carolina jasmine, ginseng, angelica, lily of the valley, and much more—species that still characterize these rich forests, though the ash, hemlock, beech, dogwood, and chestnut populations are all declining and under serious threat from exotic pests and diseases.

What have historically been known as *balds* are mountaintops that were once more open and exposed. Their origins date back to the last ice age, the Pleistocene epoch, when these high mountains were above tree line due to colder temperatures. When the climate warmed, large herbivores maintained them as balds, as did anthropogenic fire and grazing of cattle and sheep by settlers. Today a bald like Wayah would soon be grown over were it not maintained as an opening.

Section Overview

Access: To reach Wallace Branch from Porter Street/Business 441 in downtown Franklin, travel west on West Main Street, which merges with Palmer Street and then becomes Old Murphy Road. After 1.6 miles, turn right onto Pressley Road and then travel 1.7 miles to where Pressley Road merges with Ray Cove Road. The trailhead is at the end of Ray Cove Road. This is a highly popular day-use area, and parking can be difficult. There have also been some break-ins at this location, so be aware of what is visible when getting ready to leave your vehicle.

You can also access this section of trail via FS 713 at Harrison Gap. Harrison Gap is 5.5 miles from Wallace Branch. To reach Harrison Gap via FS 713, travel west on US 64 for 3.8 miles from the Franklin 441/64 intersection (Franklin bypass) and turn right onto Patton Road. There will be a sign for LBJ Job

Corps before the turn. Travel 0.2 mile and turn left at Loafer's Glory onto Wayah Road. Travel 6.1 miles and turn right onto FS 713. Travel 4.1 miles on FS 713 to Harrison Gap. FS 713 is usually closed from December through mid-March. Check the North Carolina national forests website for road closures, or call the Nantahala Ranger District at 828-524-4410.

For access to the Wayah Bald trailhead from Patton Road and Loafer's Glory, travel west 9.0 miles on Wayah Road to FS 69. You will cross the Appalachian Trail just before reaching FS 69. Turn right onto FS 69 and travel 4.1 miles to the Wayah Bald parking area. There is a Bartram Trail information kiosk along the paved trail to the summit.

This section is one of the toughest on the Bartram Trail. Starting at Wallace Branch and an elevation of 2,240 feet, the trail climbs to the summit of Wayah Bald at 5,342 feet. There is also little water after the 1.3-mile climb to Trimont Ridge. You will find a decent intermittent spring at the first Locust Tree Gap after 2.7 miles, and a reliable spring at mile 10.1 near the trail's intersection with the Appalachian Trail. Camping options are available on the first mile of the trail along Wallace Branch, but they diminish once Trimont Ridge is reached. You will see a few beyond that point, but past Harrison Gap the trail begins to ascend more steeply along the contours of Wayah Bald, and there is nothing until you reach the Appalachian Trail.

There is a chance that the trail will be rerouted from downtown Franklin up Trimont Ridge by the time this book goes to print. Check the Blue Ridge Bartram Trail Conservancy website at www.blueridgebartram.org for up-to-date info. This reroute will begin at the intersection of Harrison Avenue and West Main Street and will eliminate the Wallace Branch Road walk altogether, taking a new route up the old Trimont Ridge Trail.

Since many people choose not to take the road walks, hiking directions in this section and in the sections that follow include a second mileage number in parentheses next to the total mileage of the trail, starting with 0.0 in the first entry of this section. Lastly, there is a 50k trail race, the Naturalist, that occurs the first weekend in October. Check ahead for the exact date before planning a trip during this time.

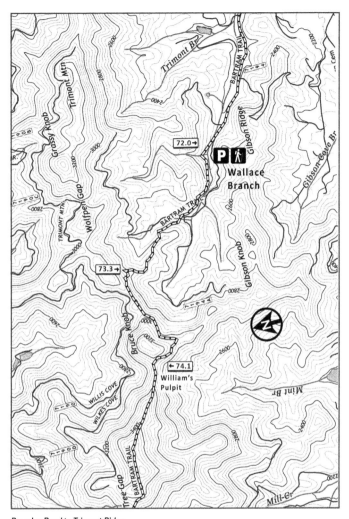

Pressley Road to Trimont Ridge

72.0 (0.0) Cross Wallace Branch on a footbridge and gradually ascend, passing a popular waterfall destination on the right
at 0.1 mile. You'll also see campsites along the west side of the
trail. At 0.6 mile cross the Forest Service road that departs on
the west side of the Wallace Branch parking area, and soon after
cross a small tributary to Wallace Branch on a footbridge. Begin
climbing up to Trimont Ridge along a spur ridge, reaching the
spine of the ridge at 1.2 miles and then Trimont Ridge at 1.3.

73.3 (1.3) Bear left onto Trimont Ridge. The old Trimont Trail, the future route of the Bartram Trail, is to the right. To the north, the community of Iotla and the Macon County Airport are visible in winter. This was the location of the Cherokee village of Jore that Bartram described as he approached the Nantahala Mountains. Much of this historically significant site is buried beneath the airport. The trail skirts the south side of Bruce Knob and

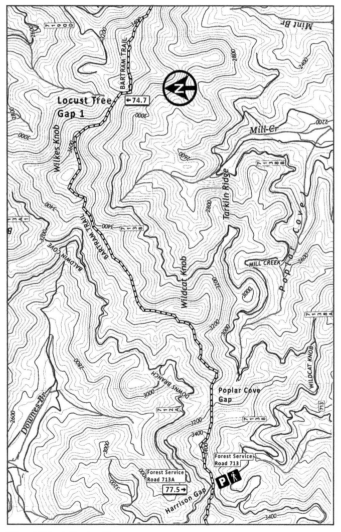

Trimont Ridge to Harrison Gap

climbs, with a hard right turn at the spine of Gibson Ridge. The trail climbs to a gap west of Bruce Knob, and then a steep climb up to William's Pulpit begins at 2.1.

74.1 (2.1) A short trail leads to William's Pulpit, a rock outcrop with excellent views to the west of Standing Indian, Albert Mountain, Siler Bald, and other Nantahala peaks. This popular day-use area can be crowded on the weekends, but past this point the number of people on the trail drops significantly. William's Pulpit bears no relation to William Bartram, who would never have considered himself a minister, but rather is named for William Haselden, a minister who was a dedicated volunteer with the trail conservancy and built and maintained many a mile of trail. From William's Pulpit, the trail continues to climb, leveling out somewhat and declining until reaching Locust Tree Gap #1 at 2.7 miles. Water and campsites are downhill to the north.

74.7 (2.7) For the next 2.8 miles the trail climbs and descends Wilkes Knob (3,640 ft) and ascends the Trimont ridgeline along the ridge (dry campsites), and then it descends to an unnamed gap before descending the north side of Wildcat Knob at 4.3 miles. The trail then climbs again, crossing the ridgeline, descends and climbs back to the ridgeline, and descends to Poplar Cove Gap at 4.9 miles (3,240 ft). This section of trail passes through a remnant stand of uncut chestnut, northern red, white, and scarlet oaks. In winter, Burningtown Gap can be seen to the northwest; it was there that Bartram turned south to climb Wayah Bald and returned to descend into the Nantahala River drainage. Travel 0.2 mile along the ridge before climbing steeply and then descending into Harrison Gap at 5.5.

77.5 (5.5) Access to Harrison Gap (3,240 ft) is explained at the beginning of this section. Camping is possible but is not advised due to local revelers frequenting the gap. A short trip down the gated Forest Service road to the north would be a much safer alternative to camping in the gap. The trail now climbs on the south side of Trimont Ridge for the next 1.9 miles, bringing you to an unnamed knob with dry campsites. The east slopes of Wayah Bald burned severely during the wildfires of fall 2016, and as a result vegetation can be very dense until you reach Wayah Bald. Canopy fires killed most of the trees, allow-

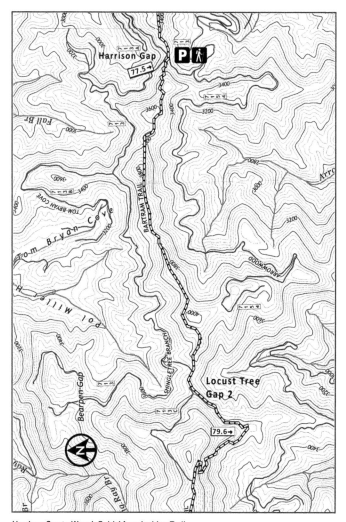

Harrison Gap to Wayah Bald / Appalachian Trail

ing much more sunlight to reach the forest floor. Maintainers cut this section as often as possible, but it can be a slog, especially in wet weather. From here the trail descends to Locust Tree Gap #2, at 7.6 miles, and you will soon see wildlife openings on the north side of the trail. Camping is possible here, though the openings are not mown often and can be densely vegetated.

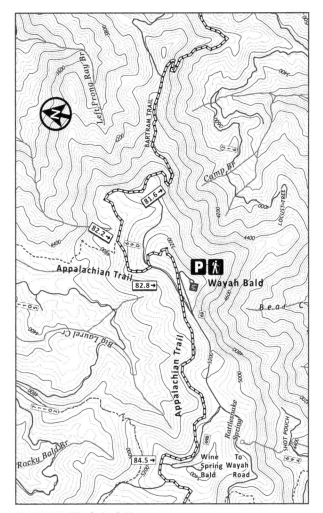

Wayah Bald to Wine Spring Bald

79.6 (7.6) Continue climbing the ridge via locust log steps in 0.2 mile, and pass a second wildlife opening at 8.7. Continue climbing a spur ridge of Wayah Bald through the burned area, reaching a fenced-off and very old mica mine at 9.4 miles. Notice the large amount of mica and quartz along the trail in this area. At this point, you will have gained almost 1,700 feet in elevation since Harrison Gap. Continue climbing the northeast side of Wayah Bald, reaching a juncture at 9.6.

81.6 (9.6) The trail ahead is used for the Naturalist race every year and leads into private property. The Bartram makes a hard right at this point and descends, then bears left at 9.9 and crosses a good water source at 10.1. At 10.2 the Bartram intersects the Appalachian Trail and makes a hard left. Camping is downhill and to the right.

82.2 (10.2) Continue uphill on the Bartram/Appalachian Trails. The Appalachian Trail is white blazed. This section of trail is rocky and botanically rich as it approaches the north side of Wayah Bald. Take note of the enormous yellow birch at 10.3. At 10.4 turn left off an old road and climb toward the summit of Wayah Bald.

At 10.8 reach the summit of Wayah Bald, which at 5,342 feet is the highest point on the Bartram Trail.

82.8 (10.8) The wooden platform at the top of the rock structure at the Wayah Bald summit was destroyed during the fires of 2016 but has been reconstructed. The fire damage to the surrounding area is apparent, and it will be interesting to see how the area recovers. Climb the firetower for one of the best views in western North Carolina.

Wayah Bald to Lake Nantahala

(7.4 MILES)

My first descent and progress down the West side of the
mountain was remarkably gradual, easy and pleasant,
through grassy open forests for the distance of two
or three miles; when my changeable path suddenly
turned round an obtuse point of a ridge, and descended
precipitately down a steep rocky hill for a mile or more,
which was very troublesome, being incommoded
with shattered fragments of the mountains, and in
other places with boggy sinks, occasioned by oozy
springs and rills stagnate sinking in micaceous earth;
some of these steep soft rocky banks or precipices
seem to be continually crumbling to earth.

Cultural and Natural History

This seven-mile-plus section represents an entry into the most
remote area of the Bartram Trail, which is relevant for those following Bartram's route and thoughts in *Travels*. Bartram's destination from Cowee was the Cherokee Overhill Towns near
modern-day Loudon, TN, which colonial traders had cautioned
Bartram against traveling to. This was the eve of the American
Revolution, and the Cherokees were engaged in skirmishes with
local settlers in this area. The guide whom Bartram expected to
rendezvous with in Cowee never showed, so Bartram decided to
proceed alone, though the colonial trader Patrick Galahan traveled with him until he began his ascent of the Nantahala Moun-

tains on an ancient trade path that crossed the mountains at Burningtown Gap. On a 1764 map made by the British cartographer Thomas Mante, this trade path is labeled *Bad Road*, and the rugged Nantahala Mountains, known then as the Jore Mountains, must have been an intimidating prospect. As noted in the previous section, Bartram's writings reveal that a certain melancholy had been building in him as he traversed the Nantahala Range, and perhaps also fear of the largely unsettled and wild landscape that lay before him.

Bartram describes reaching "the most elevated peak" of the Jore Mountains, which would be Wayah Bald at 5,342 feet, and which would have been a detour from his assumed route. Historians have speculated that he perhaps went a bit to the north of Wayah Bald and instead ascended Burningtown Bald, a lower-elevation bald that would nonetheless have offered a spectacular view. Others have theorized that he ascended an old trade path up Trimont Ridge, which the Bartram Trail now follows, and which would have taken him closer to the summit. Remnants of these trade paths remain, and both were heavily used by Cherokees and traders. Regardless, his arrival there is an important moment in the *Travels*. Bartram, upon reaching whichever of the two peaks, had never seen anything quite like the vista that lay before him. And it remains astonishing that looking west from Wayah Bald today one still sees an unbroken landscape of "mountains piled upon mountains," thanks to federal land acquisitions that created the Nantahala National Forest and the Great Smoky Mountains National Park.

Here in the rich cove forests of the Nantahala Mountains, Bartram describes seeing striped maple, white ash, black walnut, northern red oak, white oak, butternut, silverbell, viburnum, ginseng, angelica, and other species. He does not mention seeing American chestnut trees in the Nantahala, which is a bit of a mystery, though he does observe that the Cherokees used them in the construction of their homes in Cowee. Hikers on this section today will see most of these species before descending the long, narrow ridge to Lake Nantahala.

In the northwestern coves of the Bartram Trail that are shared with the Appalachian Trail, and after the Bartram leaves the Appalachian Trail and begins to wind around the northern side of Wine Spring Bald, hikers will see high-elevation species such as hobblebush (*Viburnum lantanoides*) and mountain maple (*Acer spicatum*). These two species are normally found above 5,000 feet in the southern Appalachians and are rarely seen here in the Nantahalas. They can also be found around the summit of nearby Standing Indian Mountain. In the spring, one can also find ramps, an edible and highly desirable high-elevation plant— but do not confuse this with the poisonous false hellebore, which is also found here. As the trail descends to Lake Nantahala and becomes more westerly in direction, the forests become drier, with mountain laurel, pitch pines, chestnut oaks, and dying hemlocks becoming some of the dominant forest species.

The summit of Wayah Bald is maintained as a bald through mowing and by the large number of tourists who congregate on the viewing platform and trample around the old stone firetower. The Civilian Conservation Corps built the tower in 1937. Like all Appalachian balds, Wayah Bald was likely above tree line during the Pleistocene Ice Age and was subsequently maintained over the centuries by large herbivores and through naturally occurring fires, and later through controlled burns by Native Americans and European settlers. The east side of the mountain was severely burned by the numerous arson fires that occurred in western North Carolina in the fall of 2016, resulting in crown fires on the mountain and the almost complete destruction of native trees and vegetation. One victim of the fire was an American chestnut that was fourteen inches in diameter and grew near the summit of the bald. Rhododendron and mountain laurel are returning, but so are invasive exotics such as paulownia, one of the fastest-growing trees in the world.

Section Overview

Access: For access to the Wayah Bald trailhead, from Patton Road and Loafer's Glory, travel west 9.0 miles on Wayah Road to FS 69. You will cross the Appalachian Trail just before reaching FS 69. Turn right on to FS 69 and travel 4.1 miles to the Wayah Bald parking area. There is a Bartram Trail informational kiosk along the paved trail to the summit.

82.8 (10.8) From the Wayah Bald firetower, continue down the paved path toward the parking area, leaving the path and joining the Bartram/Appalachian Trail just past the information kiosk. The two trails share the same route for the next 1.8 miles, a fact made noticeable by the presence of both yellow and white blazes on trees. The trails follow the contours of Wayah Bald, continuing around it to a point below Wine Spring Bald where the Bartram departs from the Appalachian Trail at a well-marked sign. The fires of 2016 did not reach the northwestern

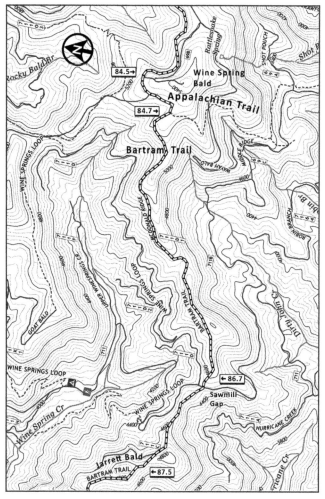

Wine Spring Bald to Jarrett Bald

slopes of Wayah Bald, and the rich high-elevation forest on this section is one of the most remarkable in the southern mountains for its plant and tree diversity.

84.5 (12.5) For those wanting to see the summit of radio-tower-covered Wine Spring Bald (5,460 ft), a blue-blazed trail on an old road here leads to FS 69B, a gravel road. Once you have reached 69B, go right for 0.2 mile to the summit. 69B is a gated road that branches off of FS 69 a mile before the Wayah Bald parking area. There is a parking area to the left of the gate.

84.7 (12.7) There is a good spring at this point, and it is the last chance for water before Lake Nantahala, which is another 5.4 miles. You will also find good campsites at this location. Just past this point the Bartram departs the Appalachian Trail to the right; a sign marks the departure. The Bartram now travels the spine of McDonald Ridge. Note the numerous hawthorns, yellow birches, and hobblebush. Over the next two miles you will encounter three wildlife openings that can be quite grown up at times, making it difficult to find the trail. You will also experience a 1,000-foot elevation loss over the next two miles. The Blue Ridge Bartram Trail Conservancy mows the trail here three times during the growing season, but it can still grow up quickly with a wet spring or summer. Keep in mind that the trail can always be found at the westernmost point of the opening. The wildlife openings do provide camping opportunities, but without easily accessible water.

86.7 (14.7) The trail descends to a gated Forest Service road at Sawmill Gap (4,542 ft). Go left and cross paved FS 711 to the parking area, where there is a kiosk with a trail map. To the right of the parking area is a gated Forest Service road where the trail resumes. The trail follows the road for the next 0.5 mile before bearing left and uphill, away from the road, onto another old logging road. This can be easy to miss, so look for yellow blazes. The trail travels uphill gradually for another 0.5 mile, gaining back almost 200 feet in elevation before skirting the south side of Jarrett Bald (4,820 ft).

87.5 (15.5) Reach the west side of Jarrett Bald. There is a decent campsite at this point, but no water source. Jarrett Bald is named for Nimrod Simpson Jarrett (1799-1871), who settled in

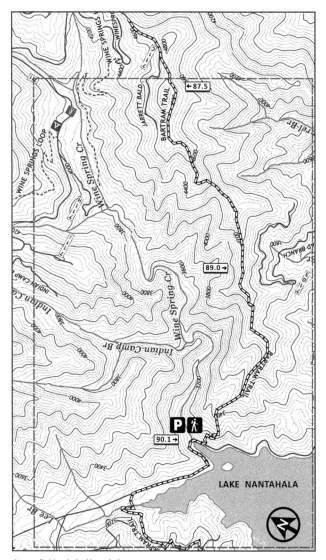

Jarrett Bald to Lake Nantahala

this part of Macon County in the early 1800s and became one of the largest landowners in western North Carolina. An enslaver, he owned mica and talc mines and was for a time one of the biggest exporters of ginseng in this part of the world. In 1871, while traveling to Franklin from his farm at Appletree, Jarrett was murdered by a Tennessee drifter named Balias Henderson. The trail begins descending steeply at 15.9, with the ridge narrowing and then widening, until the trail reaches a shallow gap at 16.8, where the trail ascends a small knoll and heads downhill. Note the large chestnut oaks along this ridge. In the winter, the views of the lake and surrounding mountains are outstanding, and even in summer there are openings where the lake can be seen. The ridgeline at certain points is choked with dead hemlocks, which have been coming down gradually over the last several years. Be cautious in high winds.

89.0 (17.0) The trail descends, steeply at times, requiring caution in the rockier sections over the next 1.1 miles, where seepage and intermittent streams make the trail slick. A small stream comes in from the right about 0.3 mile from Lake Nantahala, and the trail descends through rhododendron on steep switchbacks until reaching Wayah Road at 18.1 miles.

90.1 (18.1) The Bartram Trail parking pulloff is just to the north on the left, and additional and more spacious parking is available 100 feet down on the right, where Jarrett Creek passes under the road. Camping is possible on an old roadbed upstream.

Lake Nantahala to Appletree Campground

(5.6 MILES)

Next day proceeding on eight or ten miles, generally through spacious high forests and flowery lawns; the soil prolific, being of an excellent quality for agriculture; came near the banks of a large creek or river, where this high forest ended on my left hand, the trees became more scattered and insensibly united with a grassy glade or lawn bordering on the river; on the opposite bank of which appeared a very extensive forest, consisting entirely of the Hemlock spruce (P. abies) almost encircled by distant ridges of lofty hills.

Cultural and Natural History

The Nantahala Gorge is one of the most impressive natural areas in western North Carolina, and even with the modern-day taming of the gorge's flows and its modest development, it is easy to imagine how Bartram would have been intimidated by the rugged terrain and remoteness. The area is still one of the most remote in western North Carolina, with its narrow valleys hemmed in by National Forest lands and slopes too steep to develop. Cherokees lived in small villages in the upper reaches of the Nantahala watershed when Bartram was here, most of which are now under Lake Nantahala, but Bartram did not describe these villages as he descended the ancient path that he took down through the gorge. The area was sparsely settled, as it is to this day, and perhaps he did not notice them or consider them significant as he made his way downward "at length, after much toil and exercise."

Bartram digresses a bit from his plant obsession on this portion of his journey through the mountains, remarking instead on the geology that he encountered. He describes a "most pure and clear white earth, having a faint bluish or pearly colour gleam," which was a clay that served as a primary source of pottery material for the Cherokee. In 1767, less than a decade before Bartram's arrival, a South Carolina planter by the name of Thomas Griffiths excavated several tons of this type of clay in Cowee for the famous porcelain ceramicist Josiah Wedgwood. The exact geographic origin of that clay is uncertain, but it likely came from a cliff near what is now the Great Smoky Mountain Fish Camp, where seams of the clay are still visible. A state historical marker on NC 28 in the Cowee National Historic District documents Griffiths's visit to Cowee to mine the clay.

Griffiths's journey was a harrowing one—the Cherokees had been mistrustful since the Philadelphia Quaker and potter Andrew Duché descended upon them in 1741 with Georgia agents to look for the rumored clay. Duché had dug numerous pits looking for the clay and promised the Cherokees gifts he never delivered on. Griffiths was captured by the Cherokees for several days and described miserably wet and cold conditions in the mountains. Ironically, the same trader who Bartram befriended, Patrick Galahan, assisted Griffiths in obtaining the white clay he mined for Wedgwood. Bartram never mentions this in *Travels*, though he surely knew about Griffiths's time there.

Bartram also notes the presence of mica in the Nantahala Gorge, which the Cherokees used for ceremonial and trade purposes. Bartram describes it as isinglass and suggests that it could be used for windows or lantern glass, an observation that would become a reality a hundred years later when mica would be commercially mined throughout the Little Tennessee Valley for many uses. Heading farther down the river, he describes a new species of *Hydrastis*—or goldenseal, as it is now known. This plant's medicinal qualities are renowned, and it is rarely found in Appalachia today because of overharvesting by collectors, and because the older deciduous forests that it needs to thrive were cut over decades ago.

The area grew as settlers moved in following Cherokee removal in the 19th century, and though it was still remote and sparsely populated, it was perhaps more populated than it is today. Small communities such as Little Choga, Aquone, Beechertown, Otter Creek, and Briar Town could be found throughout the upper gorge area in the 19th and early 20th centuries. Churches, schools, stores, and logging operations dotted the landscape, and these held on until the timber ran out and the Forest Service began purchasing land during the twenties and Depression-era thirties. The removal of communities during the creation of Lake Nantahala in 1942 also had an impact. The website www.nantahalanc.com is an excellent source for photos and the early history of the area.

The area received notoricty in more recent years due to it being home to the fugitive Eric Rudolph. In 1998 the FBI identified Rudolph as a suspect in Atlanta's 1996 Centennial Olympic Park bombing and in the bombings of two abortion clinics and a lesbian bar in 1997 and 1998. The search for Rudolph was one of the most expensive manhunts in FBI history, and despite the bureau's intensive scouring of the area, he was ultimately caught dumpster diving in nearby Murphy, NC, in 2003 by a rookie police officer who had no clue as to whom he was arresting. Rudolph confessed and was sentenced in 2005 to four life sentences without parole. Attempts to prove that he was connected to militia groups in the area were found to be without merit, and today it is a peaceful and bucolic rural community where paddlers, boaters, hikers, and leaf peepers enjoy the spectacular setting.

Section Overview

Access: To reach the Lake Nantahala trailhead, travel for 17.1 miles on Wayah Road from its beginning at the turnoff from Old Murphy Road (Loafer's Glory convenience store is at this intersection). The trailhead is marked, and there is a gravel parking area on the left. There is another large parking area 100 yards down on the right. This section of the trail begins with a short walk along Wayah Road beside Lake Nantahala before turning left at an abandoned Phillips 66 station. There are NO PARKING signs posted at the station, but parking on the road is seemingly fine; multiple vehicles have parked here on Bartram Trail workdays and section hikes. The trail follows a gravel road past homes before turning left and winding back up to the old road; then it departs again into a forested landscape before intersecting the gravel Nantahala Dam Road. The trail then crosses the river at a shallow ford before picking up the gravel road that leads to Junaluska Road and Appletree Campground.

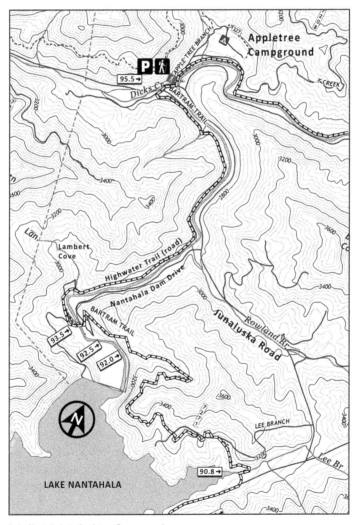

Lake Nantahala to Appletree Campground

90.1 (18.1) Travel Wayah Road for 0.7 mile, turning left at a closed Phillips 66 station onto a paved road. At 18.6 is Lakes End Café and Grill, where the thru-hiker can get a good meal from a wide selection of offerings and stock up on a few essential items. There is also a market with camping supplies. Look for a Bartram Trail sign at the old Phillips station.

90.8 (18.8) Follow the paved road, crossing Lee Branch on a bridge and then continuing along the road until turning left into recovering hardwood forest. Pay attention to blazes on this section, as there are several intersections with old roads over the next mile. At 20.0 you will see the Nantahala Dam below you.

92.0 (20.0) Follow an old road (likely used during construction of the dam) for another mile until reaching a campsite and another old roadbed. The upper Nantahala Gorge is just below, and walking upstream past the campsite will bring you to a trail that leads precipitously out to a large pool and rugged gorge cliffs created during blasting for dam construction. It is well worth seeing, but use extreme caution while skirting the bank out to the view. One can only imagine what the gorge in this area was like prior to the creation of the lake.

92.1 (21.1) Follow the old road for the next 0.3 mile, descending on a series of switchbacks through hardwood forest until reaching Nantahala Dam Road. The Bartram turns left here and crosses the Nantahala River on a concrete ford at 21.5. One can see how drastically altered the river is from Duke Energy's blasting and maintenance. To the right, Nantahala Dam Road continues for a mile before intersecting Junaluska Road. Wayah Road is 1.3 miles to the right.

92.5 (21.5) After crossing the concrete ford, walk uphill and turn right onto graveled High Water Trail Road. The Blue Ridge Bartram Trail Conservancy is working on a reroute up the mountain to the Nantahala National Forest at some future point. Check the conservancy's website for updates. Continue on the road for another two miles—paralleling the river for 0.2 mile, passing private homes and a hunt camp, and at times walking in a forested landscape without development—until reaching Cloudwalker Cove Road at 23.5.

95.5 (23.5) Turn right on Cloudwalker Cove Road, and reach Junaluska Road (SR 1400) in 0.1 mile. Turn right on Junaluska Road, and in 0.1 mile (23.7) Appletree Campground will be on your left. The trailhead and kiosk are at the entrance to the parking area.

SECTION *11*

Appletree Campground to Beechertown

(12.4 MILES)

Soon after crossing this large branch of the Tanase, I observed descending the heights at some distance, a company of Indians, all well mounted on horse back; they came rapidly forward; on their nearer approach I observed a chief at the head of the caravan, and apprehending him to be the Little Carpenter, emperor or grand chief of the Cherokees; as they came up I turned off from the path to make way, in token of respect, which compliment was accepted and gratefully and magnanimously returned, for his highness with a gracious and cheerful smile came up to me, and clapping his hand on his breast, offered it to me, saying, I am Ata-cul-culla, and heartily shook hands with me, and asked me if I knew it; I answered that the Good Spirit who goes before me spoke to me, and said, that is the great Ata-cul-culla, and added that I was of the tribe of white men, of Pennsylvania, who esteem themselves brothers and friends to the red men, but particularly so to the Cherokees, and that notwithstanding we dwelt at so great a distance we were united in love and friendship, and that the name of Ata-cul-culla was dear to his white brothers of Pennsylvania.

Cultural and Natural History

Bartram expressed relief (much as you will) following his rugged descent through the upper gorge and upon reaching the less narrow terrain of an area somewhere in the vicinity of the modern-day community of Aquone. The renowned naturalist Francis Harper speculated many years ago that perhaps Bartram traveled through Wayah Gap, where another ancient trail existed south of Wayah Bald, and came down Jarrett Creek, placing him farther south in his route into the gorge. Harper noted that mica deposits and mines in the Jarrett Creek area and Bartram's "gradual descent" in the first two or three miles of this leg of his travels give us reason to speculate. We will never know. Regardless, he was in more open country, somewhere in the headwaters of the Nantahala River. He mentions seeing the now-rare goldenseal (*Hydrastis canadensis*) in bloom, along with Fraser magnolia (*Magnolia auriculata*)—which he was somewhat obsessed with throughout his journey into the southern mountains—and describes traveling several miles over lower ridges, grassy valleys, and streams. The next day he traveled another "eight or ten miles," describing "spacious high forests" and rich soil—though Harper thought that Bartram's mileage must have been off, as it is not that far to the area now known as Beechertown, where Duke Energy's large hydroelectric plant presently dominates the landscape, along with a large parking area for commercial outfitters.

At this juncture, where Bartram describes crossing a "large branch of the Tanase," he entered a "very extensive forest, consisting entirely of the Hemlock spruce," or what is now known as eastern hemlock. One will be hard pressed to find such a forest these days, as eastern hemlocks are being ravaged by the exotic hemlock woolly adelgid, a small, introduced aphid that feeds on the tree's sap and has no natural predators in this area. There are effective treatments, though, and healthy hemlocks can still be found in some Forest Service camping and picnic areas where these treatments are being applied.

After crossing the Nantahala River, Bartram saw "a company of Indians" descending the mountains, and he immediately deduced one of them to be Attakullakulla, the grand chief of the

Cherokees, who was also known among colonials as the Little Carpenter. After Bartram and Attakullakulla extended warm greetings to each other, they talked briefly about John Stuart, the superintendent of Indian affairs, whom Attakullakulla trusted as a friend to his people, and Attakullakulla warned Bartram of troubles in the Overhill Towns, Bartram's destination. The chief welcomed Bartram to Cherokee country as a friend and brother before departing, leaving Bartram to ponder his situation.

A few months earlier, Attakullakulla and other Cherokee headmen had sold over 20 million acres of Cherokee land in Overhill country to the British. Attakullakulla's son Dragging Canoe led a rebellion against this action and began skirmishing with settlers in the area. Bartram was warned of this but continued on for another day, crossing over the Snowbird Mountains into the Valley River watershed, or perhaps more likely crossing them into the Bear Creek and Cheoah River drainage. The Valley River was settled by the Cherokees, and there were villages there during the time of Bartram's travels; the fact that Bartram does not mention seeing Indian villages lends support to the latter possibility. Regardless, he begins ruminating on the difficult landscape and slow progress, as well as the Overhill troubles, and decides to turn back. He tells his readers of an expedition into Creek country that he can join should he return to Cowee and travels back there over the next two days.

Section Overview

Access: This section of the Bartram is the longest without road access; there is no additional road access until you reach the Bartram Trail parking area at the Duke Energy power station on Wayah Road. It is also the most remote section of the trail and offers incredible opportunities for solitude and a true backcountry experience. To reach Appletree Campground, follow Wayah Road for 18.3 miles from its beginning at the turnoff from Old Murphy Road (Loafer's Glory convenience store is at this intersection) and turn left onto Junaluska Road. Appletree Campground Road is 2.4 miles ahead on the right, and the parking area for the Bartram Trail is at the entrance gate. There is an information kiosk at the parking area.

After leaving the parking area, the trail parallels the Nantahala River for the first two miles, departing from it at times and traveling up small drainages before contouring its way back down. After leaving the Nantahala, the Bartram follows an old roadbed that was built across the mountains in the early 20th century by Nimrod Jarrett, who at one time owned all the land

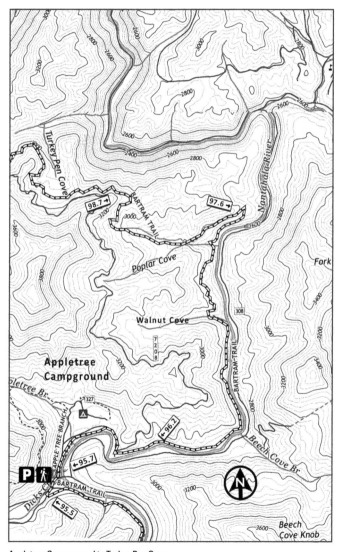

Appletree Campground to Turkey Pen Cove

in the area. Despite the length and remoteness of this section of trail, it is a relatively easy grade, without long, steep climbs or descents, until reaching the Duke Energy surge tank and the 1.3-mile walk downhill to the Bartram Trail parking area at the Duke Energy power station on Wayah Road. This section offers good water access throughout, as well as camping, though the area is rampant with wild hogs, and purification of drinking water is essential. The same gated Forest Service road that hikers pass through at Appletree Campground roughly parallels the trail for the first five miles, providing EMS access in case of emergency.

95.7 (23.7) The trail leaves the parking area and descends into dense rhododendron, paralleling the river until emerging on a Forest Service road at 23.9. Appletree Group Camp is now visible and can be busy while open, but it's empty during the winter and early spring months. The caretaker's RV can be seen up the hill. Bear right and follow the road along the fenceline, passing by a covered pavilion and picnic tables on the left. Go around the Forest Service gate and continue up the Forest Service road before taking a right back down into the forest and along the river at 24.2.

96.2 (24.2) The trail parallels the river, closely at times, for the next 1.4 miles, ascending and descending and crossing Walnut Cove Creek (at 25.8) and Poplar Cove Creek (at 26.3) on footbridges. During high water, the trail can flood in the sections that are closer to the river, leaving behind large debris piles that hikers are forced to detour around. There is one area along the river at 24.7 that can be utilized for camping, but use caution—the area burned in 2016, and there are dead hemlocks and other snags in the area, as well as downed debris. Across the river is Old River Road, which runs between Wayah Road and Junaluska Road. This area is popular for camping and is busy on the weekends. The large pipeline that runs along the river diverts water from the lake and drops it into electricity-generating turbines at the Duke Energy power station, located where the trail crosses Wayah Road near Beechertown.

97.6 (25.6) After following an old roadbed uphill along the river, the trail turns back to the left and at 25.6 begins climbing on the old road through a mixed hardwood forest and back toward

Poplar Cove Creek. This is a well-contoured section on a gentle grade, and it reaches Poplar Cove Creek at 26.0. Cross the creek, climbing the old roadbed. Cross a small stream where an old chestnut culvert was removed by a YCC Bartram Trail Conservancy crew in the summer of 2021. The old culvert sits just off the trail, just beyond an excellent campsite past the stream crossing. Prior to the removal and diversion, the stream ran directly down the trail, which can still be wet and slick with seepage. The trail continues along the old roadbed, winding its way across northeastern hardwood coves for 0.7 mile before crossing a shallow gap with potential campsites off-trail to the east on the ridge (3,040 ft).

98.7 (26.7) For the next 1.8 miles, follow the old roadbed, passing above an overgrown wildlife opening at 27.1. In early spring this area is rich with wild onion ramps (*Allium tricoccum*), giving hikers a sample of one of Appalachia's finest woodland delicacies. The Forest Service road out of Appletree is 0.2 mile up the ridge. Not far past the wildlife opening, you will pass a small creek at which serious wild hog damage is becoming apparent. Taking water from here is not advised. Continue north through rich forest coves and seepages, entering a white pine forest at 28.0 and winding down the old road until reaching Piercy Creek at 28.5.

100.5 (28.5) Piercy Creek is a wet crossing and can be high and cold at times. However, it is usually relatively shallow and thus not a difficult crossing. Rock hopping is an option in dry spells, but otherwise there is little alternative but to wade. More adventurous hikers can attempt to high-wire the rhododendron upstream, taking a chance on falling and getting wet. There is good camping at Piercy Creek. Just past the creek crossing, the Piercy Creek Trail comes in from the right (east). This 1.5-mile trail takes hikers downstream through the spectacular Piercy Creek gorge, crossing the Nantahala River at its terminus at Wayah Road. This trail is a great hike in the warmer and drier months, when wading the Nantahala River is not so daunting. The Laurel Creek Trail is 0.2 mile ahead on the left; after 1.3 miles it terminates at the Appletree Trail, which if taken to the left leads to Appletree Campground in 1.0 mile. Be aware that these trails

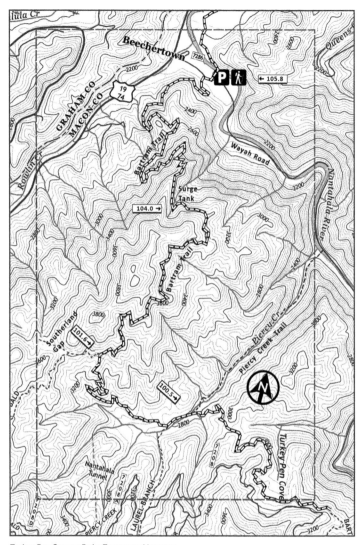

Turkey Pen Cove to Duke Energy parking area

have received minimal to no maintenance in recent years and can be impassable and difficult as a result. Continue climbing on the old road until reaching the intersection of the Bartram with the London Bald Trail. The London Bald Trail is another unmaintained trail that can nonetheless be navigated if one is skilled and unintimidated by downed trees, dense vegetation, and the lack of blazing. The trail goes for 8.5 miles before terminating at Junaluska Road (SR 1401) a few miles west of Appletree Campground.

101.6 (29.6) Leave the road, making a hard right uphill on the Bartram Trail. For the next two miles, the trail winds around the eastern slopes of Rattlesnake Knob with views of the gorge and Cheoah Bald, turning to the north and entering a botanically rich hardwood cove forest at 30.8 and crossing a narrow ridge and gap in drier ericaceous forest at 31.6. Descend for the next 0.4 mile, steeply at times, reaching the Duke Energy surge tank at 32.0.

104.0 (32.0) This vantage point offers a fantastic view of the Nantahala Gorge to the north and east. In case you're wondering, the surge tank is here to hold water during times of high-water pressure along the line passed back near Appletree Campground that is delivering water to the electric turbines below. From here the trail descends on the Duke access road. The road is gated and inaccessible to the public, so don't expect to encounter traffic. At 1.7 miles, just before the power station, the trail leaves the road to the left, passing through often dense vegetation before reaching the Bartram Trail parking area at 33.8.

105.8 (33.8) Follow the gravel road out of the parking area down to paved Wayah Road (SR 1310) and take a right. In 0.1 mile turn left into the parking area for commercial rafters. Cross the Nantahala River on a steel suspension bridge and walk for 1.2 miles on the Nantahala Bikeway/Bartram Trail, then turn left on FS 422 and cross Winding Stairs Bridge, arriving at the Winding Stairs parking area at 35.2, elevation 2,000 feet.

SECTION 12

Winding Stairs Parking Area to Cheoah Bald

(5.1 MILES)

After giving my name to the chief, requesting my compliments to the superintendent, the emperor moved, continuing his journey for Charleston, and I yet persisting in my intentions of visiting the Overhill towns continued on; leaving the great forest I mounted the high hills, descending them again on the other side and so on repeatedly for several miles, without observing any variation in the natural productions since passing the Jore; and observing the slow progress of vegetation in this mountainous, high country; and, upon serious consideration, it appeared very plainly that I could not, with entire safety, range the Overhill settlements until the treaty was over, which would not come on till late in June, I suddenly came to a resolution to defer these researches at this time, and leave them for the employment of another season and a more favourable opportunity, and return to Dartmouth in Georgia, to be ready to join a company of adventurers who were to set off in July for Mobile in West Florida.

Cultural and Natural History

Bartram was not easily intimidated by dicey situations, but his encounter with Attakullakulla clearly rattled him a bit. And it is easy to imagine that had Bartram continued to the Overhill Towns his fate might not have been a good one—and nei-

ther this guide nor the trail it follows would have been a possibility. Instead, Bartram returned to Cowee, and because of
this we have one of the only descriptions of the town's council house, which sat strikingly on top of the mound. Bartram describes the council house as a well-constructed rotunda made of
log pillars, a well-thatched roof, and seating that could hold several hundred people. He witnessed a Cherokee ritual dance per-
formance, giving a vivid account of how Cowee Cherokees were
preparing for a ball game against another Cherokee town the following day. Bartram states that such performances and dances
took place almost every night of the year in the council house,
and that a fire burned there year-round.

His descriptions of Cowee and its inhabitants are all the more
poignant given that the following year General Griffith Rutherford, in one of the early campaigns of the American Revolution,
would burn and destroy Cowee and the surrounding towns beyond recovery. During this scorched earth campaign in Septem-
ber 1776, Rutherford looted and destroyed crops, enslaved some
of the Cherokees, and drove others into the forests to forage and
starve during the upcoming winter. The campaign was based
on the fear that, since Cherokees were already skirmishing with
settlers in Tennessee and Virginia, they might ally with the British during the Revolutionary War effort, though this fear would
perhaps have been unwarranted had the Cherokees been treated
with respect, fairness, and justice in their colonial relationships.

As mentioned earlier, the Cherokee historical landscape today is being restored, as the Eastern Band of Cherokee Indians
(EBCI), Nikwasi Initiative, and Mainspring Conservation Trust
continue to acquire historically significant properties—most recently, the Watauga Mound and village site. The EBCI purchased 70 acres that included the Cowee Mound and village site
in 2007, and an adjacent 108-acre parcel in 2010. An observation platform, parking area, and information kiosk were installed
in 2020; these can be accessed by driving 7.7 miles north on NC
28 from Northeast Main Street in Franklin. An information kiosk
for the Cowee–West's Mill National Historic District is located
on West's Mill Road 6.7 miles up NC 28 from Northeast Main
Street.

The wild Nantahala gorge and river of Bartram's travels are still wild today, though less so due to the flow of the river being regulated by Duke Energy's power generation. The visual impact of the Nantahala Talc and Limestone quarry, as well as the high level of road and boat traffic, also impinges on the area's wildness. Nonetheless, the gorge would be much more developed if the owner of the quarry, Percy Ferebee, had not donated more than 5,000 acres of land in the gorge to the U.S. Forest Service in 1970. The Appalachian and Bartram Trails cross through the gorge, and the once-remote little outfitter store called Nantahala Outdoor Center, which sat at the intersection of the Appalachian Trail and US 19 when I hiked through the area as a teenager in 1977, is now a sprawling outdoor complex and the biggest employer in Swain County, NC. It is an internationally known destination, having served as the location for world canoeing and kayaking competitions.

Cheoah Bald, the Bartram Trail's terminus, is named for the Cherokee town of that name that once lay a few miles east of Robbinsville before Cherokee removal. *Cheoah* means "otter place" in Cherokee, and the nearby Cheoah River is another formerly free-flowing river altered by the creation of Lake Santeetlah in 1928 and Lake Calderwood in 1930. Restoration of the river to normal flows and releases over the last decade has resulted in the restoration of some of the river's biodiversity, along with its appeal to recreational boaters.

Section Overview

Access: To access the Winding Stairs parking area from Franklin, travel 28.0 miles on Wayah Road from its beginning at Old Murphy Road (Loafer's Glory convenience store is at this intersection). Turn right onto US 19/74, and the parking area will be one mile ahead on your right. You will pass the Duke Energy hydroelectric plant and commercial boater access parking just before the intersection at US 19. If Nolton Ridge Road (FS 259) is open, it is possible to drive within a mile of the summit and connect to the Bartram Trail at its terminus. The road is normally open in the fall for hunting season, but check with the Forest Service before planning this route. This access is made by taking US 19S for 2.1 miles from Wayah Road in Beechertown and turning right onto Tallulah Road/129 toward Robbinsville. In another 2.0 miles turn right onto Ledbetter Creek Road, and travel 0.7 mile before turning left onto Nolton Ridge Road/FS 259. Follow Nolton Ridge Road for 7.0 miles to its gated end. From the gate, walk for 0.3 mile on an old roadbed to its intersection with the Bartram Trail.

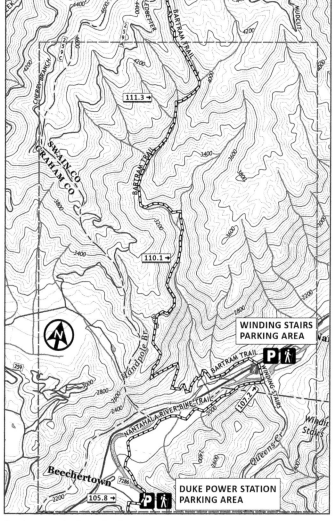

Beechertown to Ledbetter Creek

This strenuous five-mile section of trail beginning at the Winding Stairs parking area is a challenging but rewarding one, with numerous waterfalls and stunning views from the Bartram's terminus at Cheoah Bald. There is abundant water on this section until the last mile, so tank up if you are spending the night on the summit. Elevation gain is almost 3,000 feet, and this can make the climb especially difficult in the warmer summer months and extremely cold in the winter months.

107.2 (35.2) Follow FS 422 north out of the parking area, crossing US 19 and then the Great Smoky Mountain Railway before turning left onto the Bartram Trail, heading north. In 0.4 mile cross Ledbetter Creek on a log footbridge. There is good camping and water at this site. Continue climbing, moving steadily away from the Nantahala Gorge and along Ledbetter Creek's numerous rock chutes and cascades, passing campsites at 37.3 and reaching Bartram Falls at 38.1.

110.1 (38.1) Continue climbing and following Ledbetter Creek, crossing small feeder streams and seepages, occasionally with footbridges, until merging with an old road at 39.0 miles, with campsites at 39.1, and then intersecting FS 429 at 39.3 (elevation 4,300 ft).

111.3 (39.3) FS 429 is normally closed but is open during fall hunting season. Call the Cheoah Ranger District office in Robbinsville at 828-479-6431 before making plans to access the trail at this location. (See the access directions at the beginning of this section.) The Bartram Trail crosses at the end of the road and bears right, climbing up along the east side of Little Bald Mountain until reaching Bellcollar Gap at 39.8 and continuing to climb to the northeast until reaching the Appalachian Trail at 40.0 (elevation 4,800 ft).

112.0 (40.0) The Appalachian and Bartram Trails merge going east at this point. Bear right. To the left and north on the Appalachian Trail, NC 143 and the Stecoah Gap trailhead are 5.5 miles ahead. For hikers not wanting to make an in and out of this section of the Bartram Trail, it is almost the same mileage to leave a car at each trailhead and either start at Winding Stairs and end at Stecoah Gap or vice versa. Elevation gain and difficulty level are almost the same as well. In 0.2 mile reach the summit of Cheoah Bald (5,062 ft).

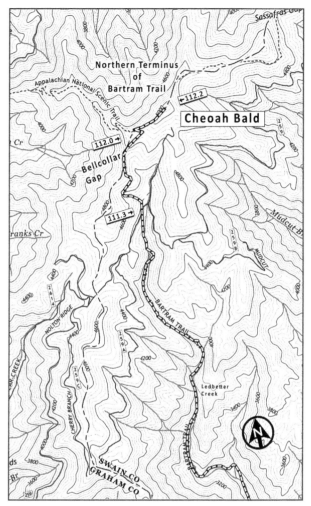

Ledbetter Creek to Cheoah Bald

112.2 (40.2) This is the end of the Bartram Trail if you're going south to north! Or the beginning if you're going north to south. Good luck! You'll enjoy incredible and expansive views to the south from the grassy opening at the summit, with great views to the north from a small bluff on the north side of the trail. There is great camping here but no water. Continuing east and south on the Appalachian Trail, Nantahala Outdoor Center is 8.1 miles ahead.

LOOP HIKES AND DAY HIKES ON
OR OFF THE BARTRAM TRAIL

Short Loop—Day Hiking

Puc Puggy, Hurrah Ridge, and West Fork Trails: (3.5 miles, moderate difficulty due to climbing and stream crossings) This figure-eight hike is great for families or for those wanting a short hike with great solitude and beautiful streams. From Osage Overlook (see section 5), go south on the Bartram out of the parking area, and in 30 feet turn left onto the Puc Puggy Trail. Puc Puggy, which translates as "flower seeker," is the title bestowed on Bartram by the Seminole people. Follow the Puc Puggy Trail for 0.8 mile until reconnecting to the Bartram, then go south (straight ahead), passing the West Fork Trail in 0.2 mile and an excellent campsite on the right. Reach the Hurrah Ridge Trail in 0.5 mile and turn left, traveling downhill for 0.6 mile to the end of FS 79. There is a rock hop across Overflow Creek just before reaching the parking area. One hundred feet down the road, the West Fork Trail goes left and mostly uphill for 0.9 mile back to the Bartram. On reaching the Bartram, turn right and hike 0.6 mile to the Osage Overlook parking area.

Long Loop—Backpacking

Bartram/Appalachian Trails: This 65-mile loop is a great backpacking trip for those who want to enjoy the beauty of the Appalachian Trail for its long Nantahala ridgeline walk and experience the remoteness and solitude of the Bartram. The trip includes the Wayah Bald and Wesser Bald firetowers, the Nantahala River at Nantahala Outdoor Center (NOC), and the summit of

Cheoah Bald. Wayah Bald, the highest peak on the Nantahala mountain range, is a great starting point, as you will lose some 3,000 feet in elevation until reaching NOC and then gain it back in the 8.3-mile hike up to Cheoah Bald. From the parking area at Wayah Bald, walk north on the shared Appalachian and Bartram Trail (see section 9) until the Bartram departs the Appalachian Trail toward Wallace Branch. Remain on the Appalachian Trail to Cheoah Bald and the terminus of the Bartram Trail. From the terminus, follow the Bartram Trail back to where the Bartram merges with the Appalachian Trail at Wine Spring Bald and then continue to Wayah Bald (see sections 9, 10, 11, and 12).

Day Hikes under Five Miles Round Trip

GEORGIA

Dicks Creek Falls—2.0 miles RT; see section 1
Martin Creek Falls—4.0 miles RT; see section 3
Rabun Bald—4.2 miles RT from Hale Ridge Road,
 1.4 miles RT from Beegum Gap; see section 4
Pinnacle Knob—4.6 miles RT from Courthouse Gap,
 8.8 miles RT from Warwoman Dell; see section 3

NORTH CAROLINA

Scaly Mountain—3.8 miles RT from Osage Overlook,
 2.6 miles RT from the Hickory Knut parking area;
 see section 5
Whiterock Mountain—4.8 miles RT from Jones Gap;
 see section 6
William's Pulpit—4.2 miles RT from Wallace Branch;
 see section 8
Wayah Bald—0.4 mile RT from the Wayah Bald parking area;
 see section 9

ADDITIONAL RESOURCES

Shuttles

Alarka Expeditions—www.alarkaexpeditions.com
Bryson City Outdoors—www.brysoncityoutdoors.com
Chica and Sunsets—www.chicaandsunsets.com
Sherpa Al, Hikers and Bikers LLC—
    Facebook page: Allen Steinman

Kayak Rentals and River Guide Services for the Little Tennessee River Section

Alarka Expeditions—www.alarkaexpeditions.com;
    alarkaexpeditions@gmail.com

Outdoor Stores

Bryson City Outdoors (Bryson City, NC)
Highland Hiker (Highlands, NC)
Nantahala Outdoor Center
    (Nantahala Gorge, Swain County, NC)
Outdoor 76 (Clayton, GA, and Franklin, NC)
Three Eagles Outfitters (Franklin, NC)
Wander North Georgia (Clayton, GA)

Art, Historical Sites, and Outdoor Activities

RABUN COUNTY, GA

Black Rock Mountain State Park, Mountain City
Chattooga River Rafting—outfitters for Sections
    III and IV: Nantahala Outdoor Center,
    Southeastern Expeditions, Wildwater LTD
Foxfire Museum, Mountain City
Hambidge Center, Rabun Gap
Main Street Gallery, Clayton
Stekoa Creek Park, Clayton

MACON COUNTY, NC

Bascom Gallery, Highlands
Cowee School Arts and Heritage Center, Franklin
Cowee–West's Mill National Historic District
Highlands Biological Station and Highlands
    Nature Center, Highlands
Little Tennessee River Cultural and Natural History
    Tours: Alarka Expeditions, Franklin
Little Tennessee River Greenway, Franklin
Nikwasi Mound, Franklin
Scottish Tartans Museum, Franklin

SWAIN COUNTY, NC

Appalachian Rivers Aquarium, Bryson City
Elizabeth Ellison Gallery, Bryson City
Fly Fishing Museum of the Southern Appalachians,
    Bryson City
Great Smoky Mountains National Park
Nantahala Outdoor Center, Bryson City—
    multiple raft and kayak outfitters, zip line park

FURTHER READING

On William Bartram

Braund, Kathryn E. Holland, and Charlotte M. Porter, eds.
Fields of Vision: Essays on the "Travels" of William Bartram.
Tuscaloosa: University of Alabama Press, 2010.

Braund, Kathryn E. Holland, and Gregory A. Waselkov,
eds. *William Bartram on the Southeastern Indians.*
Lincoln: University of Nebraska Press, 1995.

Cashin, Edward J. *William Bartram and the American
Revolution on the Southern Frontier.* Columbia:
University of South Carolina Press, 2000.

Dallmeyer, Dorinda G., ed. *Bartram's Living Legacy:
The "Travels" and the Nature of the South.* Macon,
GA: Mercer University Press, 2010.

Kautz, James. *Footprints across the South:
Bartram's Trail Revisited.* Kennesaw, GA:
Kennesaw State University Press, 2006.

Harper, Francis, ed. *The "Travels" of William Bartram:
Naturalist Edition.* Athens: University of Georgia Press, 1998.

Sanders, Brad. *Guide to William Bartram's Travels.*
Athens, GA: Fevertree Press, 2002.

Schafer, Daniel L. *William Bartram and the Ghost
Plantations of British East Florida.* Gainesville:
University Press of Florida, 2010.

Slaughter, Thomas P. *The Natures of John and William Bartram.*
Philadelphia: University of Pennsylvania Press, 2005.

Williams, Philip Lee. *The Flower Seeker: An Epic Poem of
William Bartram.* Macon, GA: Mercer University Press, 2010.

On the Region of Bartram's Blue Ridge Journey

Duncan, Barbara R., and Brett H. Riggs. *Cherokee Heritage Trails Guidebook*. Chapel Hill: Published in association with the Museum of the Cherokee Indian by the University of North Carolina Press, 2003.

Ellison, George, ed. *High Vistas: An Anthology of Nature Writing from Western North Carolina and the Great Smoky Mountains*. Charleston, SC: History Press, 2011.

Ellison, George. *Literary Excursions in the Southern Highlands: Essays on Natural History*. Charleston, SC: History Press, 2016.

Hayler, Nicole, ed. *Sound Wormy: Memoir of Andrew Gennett, Lumberman*. Athens: University of Georgia Press, 2002.

Lane, John. *Chattooga: Descending into the Myth of Deliverance River*. Athens: University of Georgia Press, 2004.

Martin, Brent. *The Changing Blue Ridge Mountains: Essays on Journeys Past and Present*. Charleston, SC: History Press, 2019.

Mooney, James. *History, Myths, and Sacred Formulas of the Cherokees*. Reprinted with a new biographical introduction by George Ellison. *Asheville, NC: Historical Images, 1992*.

Spencer, Marci. *Nantahala National Forest: A History*. Charleston, SC: History Press, 2017.